EVOLVE

STUDENT'S BOOK

with Digital Pack

Leslie Anne Hendra, Mark Ibbotson, and Kathryn O'Dell

5A

CAMBRIDGE
UNIVERSITY PRESS

Shaftesbury Road, Cambridge CB2 8EA, United Kingdom

One Liberty Plaza, 20th Floor, New York, NY 10006, USA

477 Williamstown Road, Port Melbourne, VIC 3207, Australia

314–321, 3rd Floor, Plot 3, Splendor Forum, Jasola District Centre, New Delhi – 110025, India

103 Penang Road, #05–06/07, Visioncrest Commercial, Singapore 238467

Cambridge University Press & Assessment is a department of the University of Cambridge.

It furthers the University's mission by disseminating knowledge in the pursuit of
education, learning and research at the highest international levels of excellence.

www.cambridge.org
Information on this title: www.cambridge.org/9781009235525

First published with Digital Pack 2022

20 19 18 17 16 15 14 13 12 11 10

Printed in Poland by Opolgraf

A catalogue record for this publication is available from the British Library

ISBN 978-1-009-23085-8 Student's Book with eBook
ISBN 978-1-009-23551-8 Student's Book with Digital Pack
ISBN 978-1-009-23552-5 Student's Book with Digital Pack A
ISBN 978-1-009-23553-2 Student's Book with Digital Pack B
ISBN 978-1-108-40907-0 Workbook with Audio
ISBN 978-1-108-40881-3 Workbook with Audio A
ISBN 978-1-108-41195-0 Workbook with Audio B
ISBN 978-1-108-40519-5 Teacher's Edition with Test Generator
ISBN 978-1-108-41074-8 Presentation Plus
ISBN 978-1-108-41205-6 Class Audio CDs
ISBN 978-1-108-40800-4 Video Resource Book with DVD
ISBN 978-1-009-23185-5 Full Contact with Digital Pack

Additional resources for this publication at www.cambridge.org/evolve

ACKNOWLEDGMENTS

The *Evolve* publishers would like to thank the following individuals and institutions who have contributed their time and insights into the development of the course:

Asli Derin Anaç, **Istanbul Bilgi University**, Turkey; Claudia Piccoli Díaz, **Harmon Hall**, Mexico; Daniel Martin, **CELLEP**, Brazil; Daniel Nowatnick, USA; Devon Derksen, **Myongji University**, South Korea; Diego Ribeiro Santos, **Universidade Anhembri Morumbi**, São Paulo, Brazil; Esther Carolina Euceda Garcia, **UNITEC (Universidad Tecnologica Centroamericana)**, Honduras; Gloria González Meza, **Instituto Politecnico Nacional, ESCA (University)**, Mexico; Heidi Vande Voort Nam, **Chongshin University**, South Korea; Isabela Villas Boas, **Casa Thomas Jefferson**, Brasilia, Brazil; Ivanova Monteros, **Universidad Tecnológica Equinoccial**, Ecuador; Lenise Butler, **Laureate Languages**, Mexico; Luz Libia Rey G, **Centro Colombo Americano Bogotá**, Colombia; Maria Araceli Hernández Tovar, **Instituto Tecnológico Superior de San Luis Potosí**, Capital, Mexico; Monica Frenzel, **Universidad Andres Bello**, Chile; Ray Purdey, **ELS Educational Services**, USA; Roberta Freitas, **IBEU**, Rio de Janeiro, Brazil; Rosario Aste Rentería, **Instituto De Emprendedores USIL**, Peru; Verónica Nolivos Arellano, **Centro Ecuatoriano Norteamericano**, Quito, Equador.

To our speaking competition winners, who have contributed their ideas:

Alejandra Manriquez Chavez, Mexico; Bianca Kinoshita Arai Kurtz, Brazil; Gabriel Santos Hernández, Mexico; Gerardo Torres, Mexico; Giulia Gamba, Brazil; Hector Enrique Cruz Mejia, Honduras; Jorge, Honduras; Ruben, Honduras; Stephany Ramírez Ortiz, Mexico; Veronica, Ecuador.

To our expert speakers, who have contributed their time:

Bojan Andric, Carolina Hakopian, Jacqueline Castañeda Nuñez, Lucia D'Anna, Odil Odilov, Wendy Sanchez-Vaynshteyn.

And special thanks to Wayne Rimmer for writing the Pronunciation sections, and to Laura Patsko for her expert input.

Authors' Acknowledgments

The authors would like to extend their warmest thanks to the team at Cambridge University Press. They'd particularly like to thank Gillian Lowe and Nino Chelidze for their kind, thorough, and encouraging support.

Leslie Anne Hendra would like to thank Michael Stuart Clark, as always.

Mark Ibbotson would like to thank Nathalie, Aimy, and Tom.

Kathryn O'Dell would like to thank Kevin Hurdman for his support throughout the project and for his contribution to this level.

The authors and publishers acknowledge the following sources of copyright material and are grateful for the permissions granted. While every effort has been made, it has not always been possible to identify the sources of all the material used, or to trace all copyright holders. If any omissions are brought to our notice, we will be happy to include the appropriate acknowledgements on reprinting and in the next update to the digital edition, as applicable.

Key: REV = Review, U = Unit.

Text

U1: Text from 'The Maker Movement Taking Over America. Here's How.' by Zara Stone, 11.12.2015. Copyright © Zara Stone. Reproduced with permission; **U3:** Adapted text from 'Quiet Revolution'. Copyright © Susan Cain. Reproduced with kind permission; **U5:** Wareable Ltd. for the adapted text from 'I tried VR therapy to cure my fear of flying' by Luke Johnson. Copyright © Wareable Ltd. Reproduced with kind permission; **U6:** The Moth for the text from 'Storytelling Tips & Tricks'. Copyright © The Moth. Reproduced with kind permission; MailOnline for the adapted text from 'Man trades up from a paperclip to a house', *MailOnline*, 11.07.2006. Copyright © MailOnline. Reproduced with permission.

Photography

The following photographs are sourced from Getty Images.

U1–U6: Tom Merton/Caiaimage; **U1:** Alex Trautwig/Major League Baseball; xavierarnau/E+; Mathisa_s/iStock/Getty Images Plus; MajchrzakMorel/DigitalVision; Spin12/iStock/Getty Images Plus; Steven Puetzer/Corbis/Getty Images Plus; RyanJLane/E+; stocksnapper/iStock/Getty Images Plus; Halfdark; Morsa Images/DigitalVision; Emma Farrer/Moment; TommL/E+; Hero Images; Pacific Press/LightRocket; JGI/Jamie Grill; alexsl/E+; Pekic/E+; Halfdark; kozak_kadr/iStock/Getty Images Plus; Images Of Our Lives/Archive Photos/Getty Images Plus; TonyBaggett/iStock/Getty Images Plus; SuperStock/Getty Images Plus; Michelle Bennett/Lonely Planet Images/Getty Images Plus; RyanJLane/E+; George Marks/Retrofile RF; **U2:** Tunatura/iStock/Getty Images Plus; frentusha/iStock/Getty Images Plus; Science Photo Library - NASA/ESA/STSCI/J.HESTER & A.LOLL, ASU/Brand X Pictures; Rodolfo Parulan Jr/Moment; Martín Damian Monterisi/iStock/Getty Images Plus; Jonathan Therrien/500px Prime; robas/iStock/Getty Images Plus; PeopleImages/E+; damircudic/E+; Emilija Manevska/Moment; AFP/Stringer; Wolfgang Kaehler/LightRocket; Wildroze/E+; THEPALMER/iStock/Getty Images Plus; tdub_video/E+; swissmediavision/E+; **U3:** andresr/E+; Roger Hunt/500px; Lisa Barber/Photolibrary/Getty Images Plus; sergoua/iStock/Getty Images Plus; Ekaterina Gorskikh/EyeEm; Franziska Uhlmann/EyeEm; Svetlana Zhukova/Moment; Sisoje/E+; Noah Clayton; Tara Moore/Taxi/Getty Images Plus; Ronnie Kaufman/DigitalVision; Martin Beck/arabianEye; Anthony Charles/Cultura; Jon Feingersh Photography Inc/DigitalVision; Jose Luis Pelaez Inc/DigitalVision; Francesco Carta fotografo/Moment; Seth Joel/The Image Bank/Getty Images Plus; Blair_witch/iStock/Getty Images Plus; Reinhardt Dallgass/EyeEm; kali9/E+; Patrick Frischknecht/robertharding/Getty Images Plus; H. Armstrong Roberts/ClassicStock/Archive Photos/Getty Images Plus; FG Trade/E+; Cris Cantón Photography/Moment; Ippei Naoi/Moment; Mawardi Bahar/EyeEm; Emmanuel Nalli/iStock/Getty Images Plus; Putra Kurniawan/EyeEm; Angela Bax/EyeEm; ajr_images/iStock/Getty Images Plus; Delmaine Donson/E+; **REV1:** fotoVoyager/iStock Unreleased; **U4:** Graiki/Moment Unreleased; GeorgePeters/E+; Pete Saloutos/Image Source; Klaus Vedfelt/DigitalVision; Vesnaandjic/E+; Emilija Manevska/Moment; PeopleImages/E+; Sean Gladwell/Moment; Hinterhaus Productions/DigitalVision; South_agency/E+; Michel Dória/Moment; Caiaimage/Chris Ryan; **U5:** Visual China Group; Ariel Skelley/DigitalVision; real444/E+; Luis Alvarez/DigitalVision; Asia-Pacific Images Studio/E+; FREDERIC J. BROWN/AFP; SOPA Images/LightRocket; Brent Olson/Moment; John Lamb/The Image Bank/Getty Images Plus; pbombaert/Moment; 10'000 Hours/DigitalVision; SolStock/E+; Django/E+; Hero Images; **U6:** SAFIN HAMED/AFP; Michel PONOMAREFF/PONOPRESSE/Gamma-Rapho; Idaho Statesman/Tribune News Service; Bryn Hughes Photography/DigitalVision; 5m3photos/Moment; Caiaimage/Chris Ryan/OJO+; Daniele Carotenuto Photography/Moment; kozmoat98/iStock/Getty Images Plus; Chayapon Bootboonneam/EyeEm; by wildestanimal/Moment Open; ADRIAN DENNIS/AFP; Caiaimage/Sam Edwards; Butsaya/iStock/Getty Images Plus; WHL; ilbusca/E+; Hiroshi Watanabe/Stone/Getty Images Plus; Chris Tobin/DigitalVision; Simon Winnall/Stone/Getty Images Plus; Martin Barraud/The Image Bank/Getty Images Plus; **REV2:** selimaksan/E+.

The following photographs are source from other libraries/sources.

U1: Copyright © Hailey Dawson. Reproduced with kind permission of Yong Dawson; **U6:** Dinodia Photos/Alamy Stock Photo; Copyright © Kyle MacDonald. Reproduced with kind permission.

Front cover photography by Bernhard Lang/Stone/Getty Images Plus/Getty Images.

Illustrations

U1, U3: Alessandra Ceriani (Sylvie Poggio Artists Agency); **U4:** Denis Cristo (Sylvie Poggio Artists Agency).

Audio production by CityVox, New York.

EVOLVE

SPEAKING MATTERS

EVOLVE is a six-level American English course for adults and young adults, taking students from beginner to advanced levels (CEFR A1 to C1).

Drawing on insights from language teaching experts and real students, EVOLVE is a general English course that gets students speaking with confidence.

This student-centered course covers all skills and focuses on the most effective and efficient ways to make progress in English.

Confidence in teaching.
Joy in learning.

Better Learning WITH EVOLVE

Better Learning is our simple approach where insights we've gained from research have helped shape content that drives results. Language evolves, and so does the way we learn. This course takes a flexible, student-centered approach to English language teaching.

CMBRIDGE

EVOLVE

STUDENT'S BOOK

Leslie Anne Hendra, Mark Ibbotson, and Kathryn O'Dell

5

Experience
Better
Learning

Meet our expert speakers

Our expert speakers are highly proficient non-native speakers of English living and working in the New York City area.

Videos and ideas from our expert speakers feature throughout the Student's Book for you to respond and react to.

Scan the QR codes below to listen to their stories.

Wendy Sanchez-Vaynshteyn
from Bolivia
Data scientist

Bojan Andric
from Serbia
Interpreter

Carolina Hakopian
from Brazil
Dentist

Jacqueline Castañeda Nuñez
from Mexico
Urbanist

Lucia D'Anna
from Italy
Lead Promotion Specialist

Odil Odilov
from Tajikistan
Finance Assistant

INSIGHT

Research shows that achievable speaking role models can be a powerful motivator.

CONTENT

Bite-sized videos feature expert speakers talking about topics in the Student's Book.

RESULT

Students are motivated to speak and share their ideas.

Student-generated content

EVOLVE is the first course of its kind to feature real student-generated content. We spoke to over 2,000 students from all over the world about the topics they would like to discuss in English and in what situations they would like to be able to speak more confidently. Their ideas are included throughout the Student's Book.

Find it

INSIGHT

Research with hundreds of teachers and students across the globe revealed a desire to expand the classroom and bring the real world in.

CONTENT

Find it are smartphone activities that allow students to bring live content into the class and personalize the learning experience with research and group activities.

RESULT

Students engage in the lesson because it is meaningful to them.

Designed for success

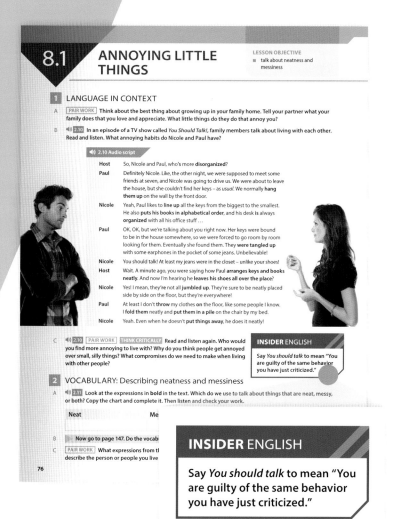

INSIDER ENGLISH

Say *You should talk* to mean "You are guilty of the same behavior you have just criticized."

Pronunciation

INSIGHT

Research shows that only certain aspects of pronunciation actually affect comprehensibility and inhibit communication.

CONTENT

EVOLVE focuses on the aspects of pronunciation that most affect communication.

RESULT

Students understand more when listening and can be clearly understood when they speak.

Insider English

INSIGHT

Even in a short exchange, idiomatic language can inhibit understanding.

CONTENT

Insider English focuses on the informal language and colloquial expressions frequently found in everyday situations.

RESULT

Students are confident in the real world.

A SMILE GOES A LONG WAY

1 READING

A Have you ever made a formal complaint? What was the problem? Was your complaint effective?

B **IDENTIFY WRITER'S PURPOSE** Read the article. What's its purpose? What specific examples of customer problems does the writer mention? Which are valid reasons for complaints?

Do you have a problem with a product, service, or company? It might be time to make a formal complaint. Anna Tims, a writer who focuses on consumer affairs, offers a list of tips for successful complaining. The secret is getting a lot of small things right.

☹ HOW TO COMPLAIN EFFECTIVELY ☹

Most large companies get hundreds of complaints – some silly and some serious. No matter how important your complaint is to you, it will just be added to a pile of complaints that a stressed-out customer service worker needs to read. So to be sure it makes the biggest impact, you must know how to state your complaint effectively. Follow these steps, and you're bound to get your problems solved.

☑ **MAKE SURE YOUR COMPLAINT IS VALID**
Your concern needs to be realistic. For example, if fees for ending a cell phone service contract early stop you from going to a cheaper cell phone service provider, that's too bad. You should have understood the contract. If, however, you have received poor service, you have the right to end your contract early. Or if you dropped your product and then stepped on it accidentally, it's your fault. But if a product breaks when you set it down gently, it's sure to be faulty.

☑ **FIGURE OUT WHAT YOU WANT TO ACHIEVE**
Do you want a refund, a replacement, or simply an apology? If you want a refund, you have to act quickly or you might lose your right to one. If you complain by phone, make a note of who you spoke to and when, and follow up the call with a letter restating your complaint and the response you got on the phone. Do the same if you sent the complaint through the company's website, so you have a record of it.

☑ **ALWAYS ADDRESS A LETTER TO A SPECIFIC PERSON**
It is best to start with the customer service manager. (If you aim too high – for example, the company president – you will be waiting while your letter is passed around until it reaches the right person.) Find out the manager's name and use their full title – Dr., Mr., Mrs., or Ms. A little thing like using someone's name can make a big impression.

☑ **INCLUDE YOUR DETAILS**
Remember to include your full name, address, and any order or reference numbers near the top of the letter. If a company can't easily find you in their system, they may not respond.

☑ **KEEP COPIES**
Make copies of all relevant documents – such as receipts, bank statements, order forms, and advertisements – and include them to support your complaint. If you want a new but stained couch replaced, include a photo of the damage.

☑ **CHECK YOUR SPELLING**
Carelessly written letters suggest you are as sloppy as the company you are complaining about.

☑ **BE POLITE AND REASONABLE**
Whether you are writing or calling, stay calm. Anger will give companies an excuse to refuse to deal with you.

☑ **NAME NAMES**
If you mention the unhelpful attitude of, for example, a store manager or customer service representative, try to include their names.

☑ **SET A DEADLINE**
Give the company a deadline for sending a useful response – 14 days is fair. Make a note of the date so you can increase the pressure if it is missed.

☑ **MAKE SURE YOUR COMPLAINT ARRIVES**
Send all letters by certified mail or special delivery so the company can't deny receiving them. If you use email, ask the person to confirm once they get it.

GLOSSARY
consumer affairs (n) a system related to protecting people who buy products and services
faulty (adj) not perfectly made or does not work correctly
sloppy (adj) not being careful or making an effort

Adapted from an article by Anna Tims in The Guardian

C Read the article again. Which points apply to (1) both a complaint letter and a phone call and (2) only a complaint letter?

D **PAIR WORK** **THINK CRITICALLY** Which three points in the article do you think would be the most effective? Why? Are there any points that won't have an effect? Why not?

2 WRITING

A Read Karen's letter to the customer service manager of Markus Appliances. What's the problem? Why is she not happy with the sales manager's response? What does she want?

To: Mr. Edwards
From: Karen Rebecca Mason
Subject: RE: Faulty SUPERWASH Washing Machine, model number RGM205

Dear Mr. Edwards,

I am writing to complain about the above washing machine, which I bought during your Summer Sale on July 15. I purchased it for $175.99 at the Main Street branch of Markus Appliances and include a copy of the receipt as proof of purchase.

After the machine was delivered, I tried to use it, but it wouldn't turn on. I checked the connection, which was fine, but the machine had no power. I immediately returned to the store and explained the problem to the sales manager, Rob Clark. At first, he suggested there was something wrong with the power in my house. When I insisted that the machine was faulty, he said, "Sorry, but you bought it during the half-price sale. We don't accept the return of sale items."

I find this unacceptable. First, the item is obviously faulty. Second, your company advertisement (copy included) states that you accept all returns without question. I believe that includes sale items. Third, I feel Mr. Clark should be friendlier. It's a small thing, but a smile goes a long way.

I would like your company to pick up the washing machine from my house and send me a refund of $175.99. I look forward to hearing from you within the next ten days.

Sincerely,

Karen Rebecca Mason

B **PAIR WORK** **THINK CRITICALLY** Which of the tips in the article in exercise 1A on page 82 did Karen follow?

C **AVOID RUN-ON SENTENCES AND SENTENCE FRAGMENTS** Read about two kinds of sentences to avoid in more formal writing. Look at the examples below. How could the sentences be improved? Then find good versions of each in Karen's letter in exercise 2A.

Run-on sentences (They go on and on.)

1 I am writing to complain about the above washing machine, which I bought during your Summer Sale on July 15 for $175.99 at the Main Street branch of Markus Appliances and for which I include a copy of the receipt as proof of purchase.

Sentence fragments (Incomplete sentences)

2 Went back to the store. Explained problem to sales manager Rob Clark.

3 Unacceptable. First, obviously faulty.

🖊 WRITE IT

D **PLAN** You're going to write a complaint letter. Choose an idea in the box or something you experienced yourself. With a partner, describe the problem and how you want the company to solve it. Then look at the letter in exercise 2A. What type of information should each paragraph contain in a complaint letter? How will you start and end the letter?

a bad restaurant meal	a broken or faulty item or package
poor customer service	an item that's different from the advertisement

E Write your complaint letter.

REGISTER CHECK

In formal written complaints, we often use expressions like *I find*, *I feel*, *I believe*, or *I think* to make statements less direct and more polite.

Direct

This is unacceptable.
Mr. Clark should be friendlier.

Less direct

I find this unacceptable.
I feel Mr. Clark should be friendlier.

Register check

REGISTER CHECK

In formal written complaints, we often use expressions like *I find*, *I feel*, *I believe*, or *I think* to make statements less direct and more polite.

Direct

This is unacceptable.
Mr. Clark should be friendlier.

Less direct

I find this unacceptable.
I feel Mr. Clark should be friendlier.

INSIGHT

Teachers report that their students often struggle to master the differences between written and spoken English.

CONTENT

Register check draws on research into the Cambridge English Corpus and highlights potential problem areas for learners.

RESULT

Students transition confidently between written and spoken English and recognize different levels of formality as well as when to use them appropriately.

"The presentation is very clear, and there are plenty of opportunities for student practice and production."

Jason Williams, Teacher, Notre Dame Seishin University, Japan

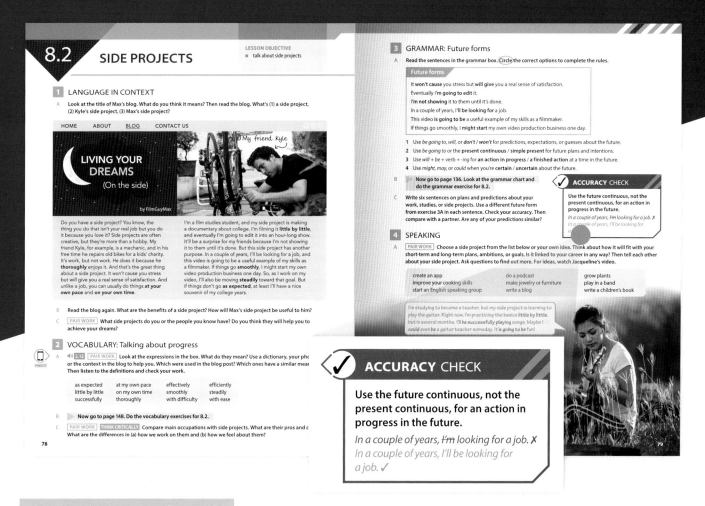

Accuracy check

INSIGHT
Some common errors can become fossilized if not addressed early on in the learning process.

CONTENT
Accuracy check highlights common learner errors (based on unique research into the Cambridge Learner Corpus) and can be used for self-editing.

RESULT
Students avoid common errors in their written and spoken English.

You spoke. We listened.

Students told us that speaking is the most important skill for them to master, while teachers told us that finding speaking activities which engage their students and work in the classroom can be challenging.

That's why EVOLVE has a whole lesson dedicated to speaking: Lesson 5, *Time to speak*.

Time to speak

INSIGHT

Speaking ability is how students most commonly measure their own progress, but is also the area where they feel most insecure. To be able to fully exploit speaking opportunities in the classroom, students need a safe speaking environment where they can feel confident, supported, and able to experiment with language.

CONTENT

Time to speak is a unique lesson dedicated to developing speaking skills and is based around immersive tasks which involve information sharing and decision making.

RESULT

Time to speak lessons create a buzz in the classroom where speaking can really thrive, evolve, and take off, resulting in more confident speakers of English.

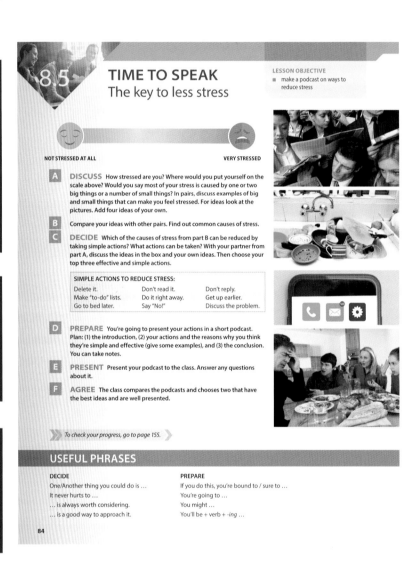

8.5 TIME TO SPEAK
The key to less stress

LESSON OBJECTIVE
- make a podcast on ways to reduce stress

NOT STRESSED AT ALL   VERY STRESSED

A **DISCUSS** How stressed are you? Where would you put yourself on the scale above? Would you say most of your stress is caused by one or two big things or a number of small things? In pairs, discuss examples of big and small things that can make you feel stressed. For ideas look at the pictures. Add four ideas of your own.

B Compare your ideas with other pairs. Find out common causes of stress.

C **DECIDE** Which of the causes of stress from part B can be reduced by taking simple actions? What actions can be taken? With your partner from part A, discuss the ideas in the box and your own ideas. Then choose your top three effective and simple actions.

SIMPLE ACTIONS TO REDUCE STRESS:

Delete it.	Don't read it.	Don't reply.
Make "to-do" lists.	Do it right away.	Get up earlier.
Go to bed later.	Say "No!"	Discuss the problem.

D **PREPARE** You're going to present your actions in a short podcast. Plan: (1) the introduction, (2) your actions and the reasons why you think they're simple and effective (give some examples), and (3) the conclusion. You can take notes.

E **PRESENT** Present your podcast to the class. Answer any questions about it.

F **AGREE** The class compares the podcasts and chooses two that have the best ideas and are well presented.

To check your progress, go to page 155.

USEFUL PHRASES

DECIDE	PREPARE
One/Another thing you could do is …	If you do this, you're bound to / sure to …
It never hurts to …	You're going to …
… is always worth considering.	You might …
… is a good way to approach it.	You'll be + verb + -ing …

84

Experience Better Learning with EVOLVE: a course that helps both teachers and students on every step of the language learning journey.

Speaking matters. Find out more about creating safe speaking environments in the classroom.

EVOLVE unit structure

Unit opening page

Each unit opening page activates prior knowledge and vocabulary and immediately gets students speaking.

Lessons 1 and 2

These lessons present and practice the unit vocabulary and grammar in context, helping students discover language rules for themselves. Students then have the opportunity to use this language in well-scaffolded, personalized speaking tasks.

Lesson 3

This lesson is built around an off-the-page dialogue that practices listening skills. It also models and contextualizes useful speaking skills. The final speaking task draws on the language and strategies from the lesson.

Lesson 4

This is a skills lesson based around an engaging reading text. Each lesson asks students to think critically and ends with a practical writing task.

Lesson 5

Time to speak is an entire lesson dedicated to developing speaking skills. Students work on collaborative, immersive tasks which involve information sharing and decision making.

CONTENTS

Listening	Speaking skills	Reading	Writing	Speaking
Upgrade ■ A conversation between two coworkers	■ Discuss issues and agree strongly	**Back to basics** ■ An article about the Maker Movement	**An opinion essay** ■ Organize information	■ Talk about your attitude toward change ■ Talk about things from when you were younger that aren't around anymore ■ Compare things in your past and present life ■ Talk about the Maker Movement **Time to speak** ■ Talk about what life was like in a past decade
Finding out ■ A conversation between a guide and a tourist	■ Exchange information	**Extreme living** ■ An interview about living in Antarctica	**A description of an area** ■ Use numerical words and phrases	■ Talk about the most important areas of research and exploration ■ Talk about life forms in difficult environments ■ Give advice on doing a free-time activity you enjoy ■ Talk about living in an extreme environment **Time to speak** ■ Plan an outdoor vacation
Asking for favors ■ Conversations between an intern, an employee, and their bosses	■ Make and respond to requests	**The right job for me** ■ An advertisement for jobs in a zoo	**A personal statement** ■ Compose and evaluate a personal statement	■ Talk about introverts and extroverts ■ Talk about how different things or experiences make you feel ■ Make and respond to requests ■ Talk about a job you would like to do and a job you would be best at **Time to speak** ■ Interview a job candidate
Two people, one job ■ A counseling session on job sharing	■ Discuss advantages and disadvantages	**The me team** ■ An article about disadvantages of teamwork	**Summary of an article** ■ Summarize main points	■ Talk about an experience of coordinating a group of people ■ Talk about making group decisions ■ Discuss advantages and disadvantages of job sharing ■ Talk about your attitude toward teamwork **Time to speak** ■ Discuss organizing a fund-raising event
Stop blaming gaming ■ A TV debate about video games	■ Consider and contrast ideas	**What language barrier?** ■ An article about translation apps	**Online comments** ■ State opinion and give examples	■ Discuss how VR programs can help people in different areas of life ■ Discuss how the development of technology can affect the way we communicate with different people ■ Discuss benefits of video games ■ Discuss translation apps **Time to speak** ■ Plan a community improvement campaign
Something in the water ■ An interview with a couple who thought they saw a shark	■ Make, contradict, and clarify assumptions	**Getting it wrong** ■ Posts about being in the wrong place at the wrong time	**A story** ■ Make a story interesting	■ Tell a story about someone who went viral ■ Talk about managing expectations ■ Describe an interesting experience ■ Talk about unexpected situations resulting from small mistakes **Time to speak** ■ Tell a story for a contest

Hailey Dawson, seven,
throwing out the ceremonial first pitch wearing a 3D-printed robotic hand at Minute Maid Park for the 2017 World Series Game 4 between the Houston Astros and Los Angeles Dodgers.

UNIT OBJECTIVES
- talk about how we deal with change
- talk about past difficulties
- discuss issues and agree strongly
- write an opinion essay
- talk about daily life in the past

STEP FORWARD

1

START SPEAKING

A Describe what you see in this picture. What do you think is special about the girl's right hand? Read the caption and check.

B In what ways can 3D-printed objects improve our lives? How might a 3D-printed object cause us problems?

C Talk about something you often use or do that has improved your life. This could be an app, a gadget, or something else.

D With a partner, list some other helpful inventions. How can they help us? For ideas, watch Jacqueline's video.

EXPERT SPEAKER

What do you think of Jacqueline's example?

LIFE CHANGES

1 LANGUAGE IN CONTEXT

A **What are some of the biggest changes that people experience in life? Are they positive or negative?**

B 🔊 **1.02** **Read and listen to an episode from Christa Garcia's podcast "No Fear." What life changes does she mention?**

🔊 **1.02 Audio script**

Ten months ago, as regular listeners will know, I made two big life changes: I moved to a new city, and I changed jobs. My work situation wasn't great: I'd just lost a job, and I couldn't find a single engineering position anywhere in Florida. Then this job in Chicago came up. It was perfect and too good to refuse. But … but … but … .

I'd lived in Florida all my life. My family was here, and my friends. And I **was frightened of tackling** a new job. Plus, it's really cold in Chicago, and this girl is 100% Florida. You know what I mean?

I said to my brother, "**I can't take** all this change!" He just said, "**Get a grip**, Christa. You're perfectly **capable of** handling all this."

After I stopped being mad at him for not being more understanding, I realized that I'm always looking for an excuse to avoid change, and I'll do anything to keep my life simple. And I'm not alone. We often talk negatively about the future, don't we? We tend to fear change. And when we're feeling scared, we **underestimate** our ability to **cope with** things. But actually, we **adapt** to new situations extremely well. Think about huge changes like starting college, getting your first job, having a baby – people **get through** challenges like this all the time. We should **accept** that we're terrific at **surviving**, and instead of **resisting** change, we should **welcome** it. That's what I did, and now life is good, and that**'s a** real **step forward**!

C 🔊 **1.02** **Read and listen again. What did Christa realize about people's ability to change? How did her own attitude change?**

2 VOCABULARY: Facing challenges

FIND IT

A 🔊 **1.03** PAIR WORK **Look at the expressions in the box. Look at how they're used in the podcast and describe each one using other words. Use a dictionary or your phone to help you. Then listen and check.**

accept	adapt	be a step forward	be capable of	be frightened of
can't take	cope with	get a grip	get through	resist
survive	tackle	underestimate	welcome	

B ▶ **Now go to page 141. Do the vocabulary exercises for 1.1.**

C PAIR WORK **Do you agree with Christa's thoughts about our ability to change? Tell your partner, and use examples if you can. Use the words in exercise 2A.**

3 GRAMMAR: Present habits

A   **Read the sentences in the grammar box. Circle the correct options to complete the rules.**

> **Present habits**
>
> I'm **always looking for** an excuse to avoid change, and I'**ll do** anything to keep my life simple.
>
> We **often talk** negatively about the future, don't we?
>
> We **tend to fear** change.
>
> When we'**re feeling** scared, we underestimate our ability to cope with things.

1   For a habit that is more noticeable or frequent than usual, you can use *always* or *constantly* with the **simple present / present continuous**.

2   You can use the modal *will* for **present / past** habits.

3   You can use the verb **tend to / keep** + a verb to talk about present habits.

4   You can use the **simple present / present continuous** for a continuing activity that happens at the same time as another habit.

B   **Now go to page 129. Look at the grammar chart and do the grammar exercise for 1.1.**

C   PAIR WORK   **Think of something you do regularly, such as going to the gym, meeting friends, studying, or working. Describe your present habits using the prompts below. Then compare your sentences with a partner. How different or similar are your regular habits?**

1   I tend to …

2   My friends and I often …

3   When I'm feeling …

4   I'm always …

5   When I'm tired, I'll …

D   **Think of one thing you'd like to change about your life. What habits do you have that prevent you from moving forward? How can you tackle these habits?**

4 SPEAKING

A   GROUP WORK   THINK CRITICALLY   **Do you welcome change, or do you prefer to stick to your habits? Explain your answers. Is it easier to adapt to changes that you decide to make or ones that are outside your control? Think of some examples.**

> I **tend to worry** about big changes. I'**ll follow** the same routine every day and be perfectly happy about it. I think things outside our control, like losing your job or your best friend moving away, are harder to **cope with** because you can't plan and prepare for them.

3

1.2 MEMORY LANE

1 LANGUAGE IN CONTEXT

A PAIR WORK Look at the pictures. When were the items popular? When did people stop using these items? Why?

B Read Amy's blog post. What time period does she describe? How old do you think she was then? How old is she now?

banana seat bike

The TIME MACHINE in my living room

wall phone with a cord

TV with no remote control

Do you ever binge-watch TV shows and feel like you've taken a time machine to a different place and time? I just watched *Stranger Things*, which takes place in the 1980s. It was like going back in time to my childhood.

Remember those bikes with banana-shaped seats? One of the boys in the series rides one, just like the one I used to ride to school every day. I wouldn't even lock it – I'd just leave it outside all day. In many ways, life was simple then. But some things were **frustrating** …

When you're on the phone, do you move around a lot, like me? Well, in the 1980s, we could only walk as far as the cord reached. And with only one phone in the house, we didn't use to have any privacy. I'd **drive** my brother **crazy** because I talked to my friends for hours. Making calls away from home was **tricky**, too. Have you ever used a pay phone? I never used to have enough coins with me – it was **infuriating**! And how about sharing music? You probably use a music app, right? My older sister used to make me mixtapes with different songs she liked. I realize now how **complex** and **time-consuming** it was. Even watching TV was more difficult then. It **got on my nerves** to have to get up and change the channel all the time because there was no such thing as a remote control. Now I just push the "off" button from the couch to travel back to the present and take a break from binge-watching!

cassette tape

GLOSSARY
binge-watch (v) to watch many or all episodes of a TV show in one session

2 VOCABULARY: Describing annoying things

A Cover the blog post. Can you remember which seven words and phrases from the box below Amy uses? What does she describe with the words?

awkward	be a waste of time	be hard to operate	clumsy	**!** sb = somebody
complex	drive sb crazy	frustrating	get on sb's nerves	
infuriating	lose patience	time-consuming	tricky	

FIND IT

B ◄)) **1.04** Look at the words in the box again. Which ones are adjectives, and which ones are verb phrases? Use a dictionary or your phone to help you. Then listen and check. Which words mean *annoying*? Which mean *difficult, uncomfortable, takes a lot of or too much time*?

C ▶ Now go to page 141. Do the vocabulary exercises for 1.2.

D PAIR WORK THINK CRITICALLY Describe some present-day everyday objects using words from exercise 2A. Which of them do you think will still be used in ten years' time? How might they change?

3 GRAMMAR: Past habits

A Read the sentences in the grammar box. Circle the correct options to complete the rules. Can you find more examples in the text in exercise 1B on page 4?

> ### Past habits
>
> We **didn't use to have** any privacy.   I **never used to have** enough coins.
> I**'d drive** my brother crazy.
> It **got** on my nerves to have to get up and change the channel all the time.

> **!** Use the simple past for single completed past actions:
> *I just **watched** the last episode of Stranger Things.*

1 *Used to*, *didn't use to*, and *never used to* can show past habits, **single / repeated** past actions, and past states.

2 *Would (not)* can mean the same thing as (**not**) *used to* / **could** (*not*) for past habits and repeated actions. Do not use *would (not)* for past states.

3 You **can / can't** use the simple past for past habits, repeated past actions, and past states.

B ▶ Now go to page 129. Look at the grammar chart and do the grammar exercise for 1.2.

C Change the sentences so they're true for you. Use (*not/never*) *used to* or *would (not)*. Then check your accuracy. Compare your statements with a partner.

1 When I was a child, I rode my bike without a helmet.

2 My parents cooked with a microwave.

3 I didn't stream music in the 1990s.

4 When I was a kid, I texted my friends every day.

5 Before cell phones, I had to memorize my friends' phone numbers.

> ✓ **ACCURACY** CHECK
>
> Do **not** use *be* before *used to* when talking about past habits.
> *I ~~am~~ used to cycle to school.* ✗
> *I used to cycle to school.* ✓

4 SPEAKING

A [PAIR WORK] Think of objects from when you were younger that aren't around anymore. Why aren't they around anymore? Do you miss those objects? Why or why not? For ideas, watch Jacqueline's video.

> I **used to have** this game console that fit in my pocket. It only had one game, but I**'d carry** it around everywhere and play the game all the time. It was really **frustrating** if I forgot to bring it with me. Now I simply play games on my phone …

EXPERT SPEAKER

How similar are Jacqueline's memories to yours?

1 LISTENING

A **PAIR WORK** In what situations do you send or receive emails? Do you think it's an effective way to communicate? Why or why not?

B 🔊 **1.05** Listen to coworkers Shawn and Lorena talk about problems with email. What other ways of communication do they mention?

C 🔊 **1.05** **LISTEN FOR OPINIONS** Listen again. What does Lorena think the problems with email are? Do you agree with her? What does Shawn think about the alternative that Lorena mentions? Do you agree with him?

D **PAIR WORK** **THINK CRITICALLY** Compare different ways of communication, such as face-to-face conversations, texts, IMs, video calls, etc. What are their advantages and disadvantages? Which ways of communication do you find most effective in which situations?

Shawn Harvey
Managing Director

Lorena Cook
Team Leader

2 PRONUNCIATION: Listening for main stress

A 🔊 **1.06** Listen. What do you notice about the underlined words?

1 … I can get some <u>real</u> work done.

2 … people usually choose the <u>easy</u> option.

3 All this technology was supposed to help us be more <u>efficient</u> …

B 🔊 **1.07** <u>Underline</u> the word in each item that you think has the main stress. Listen and check.

1 When it comes to technology, …

2 … waiting to use the single fax machine we had in our office.

3 And don't forget about all that paper!

C ⭕Circle the correct words to complete the sentences.

One word / Several words in each word group will have the main stress. Words with the main stress are usually near the *beginning / end* of the word group, and they give information that is *new (and important) / old (and not so important)* to listeners.

INSIDER ENGLISH

When something used to connect to the internet isn't working, it's "down."

*It looks like the server is **down**.*

*My Wi-Fi is **down** again!*

3 SPEAKING SKILLS

A 🔊 **1.05** Look at the sentences from the conversation in exercise 1B on page 6. Are the speakers discussing issues (D) or agreeing strongly (A)? Write *D* or *A*. Where, do you think, is the main stress in each sentence? Listen to the conversation again to check.

> **Discuss issues and agree strongly**
>
> 1 **When it comes to** technology, you can rely on the server to be unreliable. ___
> 2 **That's so true!** ___
> 3 **You can say that again.** ___
> 4 **I couldn't agree more.** ___
> 5 **Looking at the big picture**, I think email isn't that bad. ___
> 6 **Overall**, if I had to choose … ___
> 7 **Have it your way!** ___

B PAIR WORK **With your partner, take turns making and responding to statements using the prompts below and bold expressions from exercise 3A.**

1 writing / easier / laptop / tablet
2 texting / the best way to communicate with …
3 video calls / for work / personal communication
4 face-to-face / most important for …

C ▶ PAIR WORK **Student A: Go to page 157. Student B: Go to page 158. Follow the instructions.**

4 PRONUNCIATION: Saying /ʧ/

A 🔊 **1.08** Listen to the /ʧ/ sound in these words and then repeat the words.

pic<u>tu</u>re   <u>ch</u>eap   sugges<u>ti</u>on   a<u>ch</u>ieve   tou<u>ch</u>   ques<u>ti</u>on

B <u>Underline</u> **the /ʧ/ sound in each pair of words.**

status   statue   stomach   watch   actual   action   nature   major

🔊 **1.09** **Listen and check. Then repeat the words with the /ʧ/ sound.**

C <u>Underline</u> **the /ʧ/ sounds in the conversation below. Then take turns practicing the conversation with a partner.**

A Looking at the bigger picture, we've got more of a chance now.
B Actually, I don't think we're going to achieve very much. We need to make some big changes.

5 SPEAKING

A GROUP WORK **Compare something from your past with something in your present life. Look at the ideas below. Discuss your views on the issues.**

last job / current job   high school / college
last home / current home   old device / current device

> Generally speaking, I think the atmosphere in college is more relaxed than in high school.

> I couldn't agree more.

> So, **overall**, do you think college is easier?

A · **IDENTIFY MAIN IDEAS** What skills or knowledge have your grandparents and parents passed on to you? Can you tell your partner something that you do or make that they taught you? Read the article and say what Barbara's grandparents passed on to her. What is the Maker Movement?

COMING AROUND AGAIN

When I was a kid, I used to spend weekdays with my grandpa and grandma while my mom was at work. I'd sometimes help my grandma make her special oatmeal cookies. To be honest, I used to be better at eating them than I was at baking them. They were so good! But in those days, more often than not, I'd watch my grandfather in his workshop – actually their garage – where he spent most mornings. He was an amateur inventor, and he would take old pieces of metal or wood and make something new and practical that he or my grandmother could use around the house. He once gave me a wallet to hold dollar bills that he had made out of flat cardboard, leather, and elastic. It was a magic wallet – you opened the wallet, placed the bill on top of the elastic inside, closed the wallet, opened it again from the other side and – lo and behold – the bills were behind the elastic and held securely. He had put a ten dollar bill in there, "just in case you need it." Every time I use it I think of my grandfather, and I know it's the only wallet in the world like it.

Fast forward to earlier this year. I went to a Maker Faire with my friend. "What's a Maker Faire?" I hear you ask. Well, first I need to tell you about the Maker Movement. This was founded way back in 2005 as a way to encourage DIY through art, electronics, and craft projects. Since then, it's gone from strength to strength around the

world. There are about 135 million makers in the U.S. alone – that's over half the population. Maker Faires are basically festivals which celebrate and promote these skills. The 2015 Maker Faire had over 1.1 million visitors – the same audience size as Taylor Swift's *1989 World Tour*.

So, how is the Maker Movement different to what my grandpa was doing in his workshop all those years ago? It's hard to define, but a lot of it is about individuals using new technologies – technologies that are accessible to you and me, like 3D printers – so that they can create unique items and projects that have a use beyond their original intention. A maker is anyone who is creating, and if you're building or adapting something or trying to make something new, that means you.

The future could be pretty exciting for all makers out there. Dale Dougherty, founder of Maker Media which published *Maker: Magazine* back in 2005, and that kicked off the movement, believes the future of makers depends on education. He says young people need help to develop their creative and technical abilities. "When kids play *Minecraft* they expect not just to play, but also to evolve," Dougherty said. It's fun, and everyone tackles projects and learns skills together.

My grandparents are gone now, but I'd love to think that if they were around today they would be makers, too. I've inherited my grandfather's love of finding out how things work, and I've just sold my first handmade lamp that I made from recycled glass and other materials. By using the creative skills they passed down to me, in my own way I've joined the maker movement.

By Barbara Cohen

GLOSSARY
amateur (*adj*) doing something as a hobby
craft (*n*) an activity in which you make something using a lot of skill, especially with your hands
DIY (do-it-yourself) (*n*) repairing and making things yourself instead of paying someone to do it

B · **IDENTIFY SPECIFIC INFORMATION** Read the article. What's the significance of these numbers?

a 2005 b 135,000,000 c 2015 d 1,100,000

C · **THINK CRITICALLY** Why do you think the Maker Movement has become so popular around the world? What do you think of this movement? Would you be interested in becoming a maker?

2 WRITING

A Read Carmen's essay about forgotten skills. Which ones does she mention? What was good about them?

Reviving forgotten skills

Recently, there has been some discussion about reviving skills from the past, such as repairing mechanical items like watches and raising animals. These skills are good for the environment, save money, and can be extremely enjoyable. I think this is an excellent trend and would like to share two almost-forgotten skills that my grandmother used to have.

The first is sewing. Most of us buy our clothes at the store, and we throw them away when they're worn. My grandmother, however, used to make clothes for my father, and later in life for my sisters and me. She would fix holes and small tears in our clothes, too, so they would last until we grew out of them.

The second skill is preserving food. My grandmother used to preserve all kinds of fruit and vegetables in the fall and store them in jars. Then, in the middle of the winter, she'd bring out a jar of raspberries or cucumbers, and it would immediately bring back a wonderful feeling of summer. It also cost less than buying them in the store.

I think bringing back skills like these is a fantastic idea. In fact, I'm planning to research how to raise chickens so I can have fresh eggs.

GLOSSARY
revive (v) to make something from the past exist again
preserve (v) to treat food in a particular way so it can be kept for a long time

B **ORGANIZE INFORMATION** Read about organizing an opinion essay. Then check if Carmen's essay has all these features.

1st paragraph: Introduce the topic and state your opinion.

2nd paragraph: Use a topic sentence to introduce your example and give the main idea of the paragraph; describe the example.

3rd paragraph: (same as second paragraph)

4th paragraph: Restate your opinion but with different words than before.

WRITE IT

FIND IT

C **PLAN** You're going to write a formal opinion essay about skills from the past. With your partner, discuss two or three forgotten skills and what you would like to say about them. Choose from the skills in the pictures below or use your phone to find other ideas. Then think how you will organize your essay, using the structure described in exercise 2B. What points are you going to include in each paragraph?

D Write your opinion essay. You can write a similar introduction and conclusion to Carmen's.

knitting

baking

beekeeping

making pottery

E **PAIR WORK** Read your partner's essay. What do you think of the skills he or she describes?

1.5

TIME TO SPEAK
Blast from the past

| 1910 | 1920 | 1930 | 1940 | 1950 | 1960 | 1970 | 1980 | 1990 |

A **PREPARE** Look at the pictures. In pairs, discuss which decade you think each picture is from. Then work with another pair and discuss your ideas. How else was life different in each time period?

B **DECIDE** Imagine you are on a reality TV show where you have to live for a week the way people did in the past. In groups, say which decade you want to live in, from 1910 to 1990, and why. Then decide on one decade together.

FIND IT

C **RESEARCH** In your group, answer the questions about what life was like in the decade you chose. You can go online to research ideas.

1 How did people use to do everyday chores?
2 What transportation did they use?
3 What styles of clothes did they wear?

4 What tech items did they have?
5 How did they entertain themselves?

D Imagine you just finished your week on the TV show. In your group, talk about your imagined experiences. How does living in that decade compare to life today? What was better? Worse? What did you enjoy about the experience? What difficulties did you have?

E **DISCUSS** You are going to debate whether it's better to live now or in the decade you discussed. Make two teams within your group. Team A: Think of reasons why life was better then. Team B: Brainstorm the reasons why it's better to live in the present day. Each team has two minutes to present their points to the other team.

F Report the results of your debate to the class. Would most people prefer to live in the past or now?

To check your progress, go to page 153.

USEFUL PHRASES

PREPARE

It was very awkward.
It was hard to operate.
It used to drive … crazy
It was really tricky.

DISCUSS

It was a step forward from …
We shouldn't underestimate …
It helped to cope with …
It was a waste of time.
It used to be so time-consuming.

Generally speaking, …
Looking at the big picture …
Overall …
When it came to …

UNIT OBJECTIVES

- talk about exploration and research
- talk about life forms in different environments
- exchange important information
- write a description of an area
- plan an outdoor experience

NATURAL LIMITS

2

START SPEAKING

A   What can you see in the picture? What effect do you think it has on the fish and other wildlife in the ocean?

B   In what other ways does human activity affect wildlife? Can you think of examples from your area or country?

C   What are the benefits and drawbacks of human activity you discussed in exercise B? Do you think the activity is justified? For ideas, watch Odil's video.

EXPERT SPEAKER

What do you think of Odil's ideas?

DEEP OCEAN OR DEEP SPACE?

1 VOCABULARY: Space and ocean exploration

A Look at the pictures. Which one is in space? Which is in the ocean? Which do you think most people would want to learn about?

B ◀) **1.10** PAIR WORK Look at the words and phrases in the box and discuss their meanings. Use a dictionary or your phone to help you. Then listen and check your work. Which words and phrases could you use to talk about space, which about the ocean, and which about both?

atmosphere	come across	exploration	investigation
launch	monitor	observe	preserve
resources	satellite	species	surface
use up			

A An amoeba

B A supernova

C ▶ Now go to page 142. Do the vocabulary exercises for 2.1.

D PAIR WORK THINK CRITICALLY Why do we explore space and the ocean? What effect can it have on our daily lives? Are there other issues we should be using our resources on instead?

2 LANGUAGE IN CONTEXT

A ◀) **1.11** PAIR WORK Read and listen to the podcast. What are the advantages and disadvantages of space and ocean exploration according to the speakers? Which speaker do you agree with more. Why?

◀) 1.11 Audio script

Host Today's guests on *Discovery Now*, Ronnie Jones and Johanna Flores, are here to discuss the question: Which is more important, space or ocean **exploration**? Ronnie?

Ronnie I would definitely prefer to explore space rather than study the ocean. There's so much mystery beyond Earth's **atmosphere**. And we can learn more from research into space than most people realize. Without it we would probably never have inventions like phone cameras, ear thermometers, wireless headsets, and even clean energy technology.

Johanna I disagree. How about the benefits of underwater research for industry, for medicine, for technology? And it's much less expensive and a lot safer than space travel. Space exploration just isn't useful enough to justify the cost.

Host Good point. Can you justify the cost, Ronnie?

Ronnie Of course. The earth is getting overcrowded, and it won't be long before we'll need other places to live. Solving future problems on Earth is worth any price.

Johanna It's less important to fix future problems than to fix current ones. People depend on the ocean for jobs, food, and even breathing! Ocean plants produce about 70 percent of Earth's oxygen. Maybe we should find ways to **preserve** our oceans' **resources** instead of **using** them **up** – which is a lot easier than trying to live in space.

Ronnie But what about life in space? On Mars, for example, there's water, and where there's water, there could be life!

Johanna But we don't know for sure if any other planets support life. However, there's definitely life below the **surface** of the ocean we still know almost nothing about. We keep discovering amazing **species** deep under the water. Only about five to ten percent of the deep ocean has been explored. Overall, it is obvious to me that there are fewer benefits to space exploration.

3 GRAMMAR: Comparative structures

A Read the sentences in the grammar box. (Circle) the correct options to complete the rules.

> ### Comparative structures
>
> I would definitely prefer to explore space **rather than study** the ocean.
>
> We can **learn more** from research into space **than** most people realize.
>
> Space exploration just **isn't useful enough** to justify the cost.
>
> It's **less important to fix** future problems **than** (it is) **to fix** current ones.
>
> There are **fewer benefits** to space exploration.

1   When comparing, put the thing you like less after **prefer / rather than**. To compare actions, use a gerund or the **base form of the verb / past participle** after *rather than*.

2   When using *more* or *less* as a pronoun, put it **after / before** a verb.

3   Use **a gerund / an infinitive** after an adjective + *enough*.

4   Use *less* with **count / non-count** nouns. Use *fewer* with **count / non-count** nouns.

5   You **always have to / don't always have to** repeat the first subject + verb in comparative structures.

B   ▶ **Now go to page 130. Look at the grammar chart and do the grammar exercise for 2.1.**

C   Complete the sentences with your own ideas using the constructions in parentheses. Then check your accuracy. Compare ideas with a partner.

1   Ocean exploration is … (adjective + *enough* + infinitive)

   Ocean exploration is not important enough to justify the risks.

2   Space travel is … (adjective + *enough* + infinitive)

3   Space exploration is … (comparative adjective + *than*)

4   I prefer … (verb/gerund + *rather than* + verb/gerund)

5   We can learn … (*more* or *less* as a pronoun)

6   It's less important … (infinitive *than* infinitive)

> ✓ **ACCURACY** CHECK
>
> Use *than*, not *then*, with comparative structures.
>
> *There is less oxygen on Mars ~~then~~ on Earth.* ✗
>
> *There is less oxygen on Mars than on Earth.* ✓

4 SPEAKING

A   THINK CRITICALLY **What environments do people explore? What do you think are the top areas of research and exploration that can help us and the planet? Why? For ideas, watch Odil's video.**

> People explore the natural world around them and also their own biology. It may be **easier to solve** our most urgent issues by **observing** the results of human activity or studying our DNA, **rather than trying** to **investigate** …

EXPERT SPEAKER

Do you think Odil's suggestions are good? Why or why not?

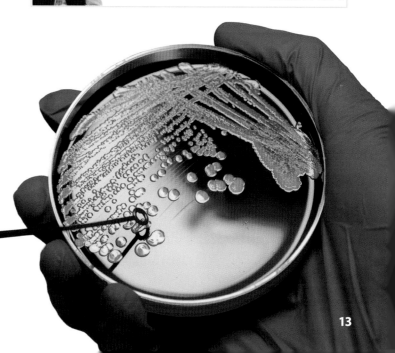

2.2 EXTREME LIFE

LESSON OBJECTIVE
- talk about life forms in different environments

1 LANGUAGE IN CONTEXT

A   PAIR WORK   Make a list of ten wild animals in your country. Where can you usually find them? Does your country have an official national animal?

B   Read the article about four unusual animals. What are they? Where do they live?

NATURE'S "TOUGH COOKIES"

We often discuss how to preserve **endangered** species of wildlife but rarely talk about the opposite side of nature: **creatures** that can survive in extremely difficult **environments**. So here are four examples of nature's "tough cookies."

Nicaragua's Masaya Volcano is one of the most active **volcanoes** in Central America. **Poisonous** gas rises from the volcano. It's an absolutely awful place to live. Yet hundreds of small, green parrots have made it their home. Experts aren't sure how they survive in a **habitat** that would kill other **forms of life**, but somehow they've managed to adapt to it.

In Alaska, where temperatures remain below zero for several months, wood frogs survive by freezing. Almost two-thirds of their body water turns to ice. They become very hard and appear to be dead. But in the spring, they thaw out and head straight for the nearest **pond**.

Super-hot water and poisonous gases boil up from holes in the ocean floor off the coast of Ecuador. This is surely the least suitable environment for anything to live. Yet in and around these holes, various forms of **sea life** exist. The tiniest and most common are microbes called "extremophiles." Their existence may help explain the **origins** of life on earth.

The final "tough cookie" has few limits to its **territory**. Rats are the most **adaptable** mammal that we know of. They live almost everywhere and recover fast from whatever we do to them. They won't win a popularity contest, but they definitely get the first prize for being super **survivors**.

GLOSSARY

head (straight) for (v) go toward something

microbe (n) a very small living thing that can only be seen with a microscope

mammal (n) an animal that feeds its babies milk

C   Read the article again. What makes each living thing a "tough cookie"? Which one do you think is the toughest? Why?

2 VOCABULARY: The natural world

INSIDER ENGLISH

Someone is a *tough cookie* if they are not easily hurt emotionally or physically.

You don't need to worry about Rachel. She is a really tough cookie.

A   🔊 1.12 Look at the words in the box. Which two are not in the article? Which ones are nouns or noun phrases, and which are adjectives? Listen and check your work.

adaptable	animal life	creature	endangered	environment
form of life	habitat	origin	plant life	poisonous
pond	sea life	survivor	territory	volcano

B   ▶ Now go to page 142. Do the vocabulary exercises for 2.2.

C   THINK CRITICALLY   What are some endangered animals that you know of? What do you think can be done to protect them?

3 GRAMMAR: Superlative structures; ungradable adjectives

A Read the sentences in the grammar boxes. (Circle) the correct options to complete the rules.

Superlative structures

Nicaragua's Masaya Volcano is **one of the most active** volcanoes in Central America.

Yet in and around these holes, various forms of sea life exist. **The tiniest and most common** are microbes.

Rats are **the most adaptable** mammal (that) we know of.

Ungradable adjectives

It's an **absolutely awful** place to live.

They become very hard and appear to be **dead**.

The **final** "tough cookie" has few limits to its territory.

1 After *one of the most* + adjective, use a **singular / plural** noun.

2 Nouns are not always repeated after superlative adjectives. After "the tiniest and most common," the missing words are *holes / forms of sea life*.

3 For superlative structures with *that* clauses, *that* is **always / not always** needed.

4 You **can / can't** use ungradable adjectives with *absolutely* and *completely*.

B ▶ **Now go to page 130. Look at the grammar chart and do the grammar exercises for 2.2.**

C Complete the sentences about the natural world. Compare with a partner. Answers are at the bottom of the page.

1 The black mamba is one of the most poisonous _____ .

2 The dwarf lantern shark is one of the _____ animals in the ocean.

3 Out of all the planets in the solar system, Neptune and Uranus are the _____ .

4 The water in the geysers can be very hot or even absolutely _____ .

4 SPEAKING

FIND IT

A PAIR WORK Choose one of the topics below. Where can these life forms be found? How difficult is life for them? You can check online if you want. Then tell another pair about the topic you chose.

- wild animals that have adapted to life in your city
- the rarest animals, birds, or plants in your country / the world
- the most beautiful or the most dangerous forms of life you know of

> One of the most common wild animals in our city is the raccoon. A common habitat of urban raccoons are people's sheds and attics. Raccoons come out into the streets to find food, but city life is extremely dangerous for them …

Answers: 1 snakes 2 smallest 3 coldest or farthest from the sun 4 boiling

2.3 FINDING OUT

1 LISTENING

A PAIR WORK Do you think hiking is a fun activity? Why or why not? Tina is preparing to go hiking in the mountains of Peru. She calls her guide to ask about things she needs to take with her. Imagine you're Tina. Think of some important questions to ask.

B 🔊 1.13 Listen. What are the four different problems with water and sweat that the guide discusses?

C 🔊 1.13 LISTEN FOR DETAILS Listen again. Complete the information that the guide provides.

1 Type of coat to bring: _____

2 Type of T-shirt <u>not</u> to bring: _____

3 Minimum size of backpack: _____ liters

4 Weight of backpack without water: _____ kilos

5 Weight of water: _____ kilos

D In your opinion, which of the water problems described by the guide is the most dangerous? Explain why.

2 PRONUNCIATION: Listening for weak forms and rhythm

A 🔊 1.14 Listen to the phrase *a couple of questions*. What pattern does it have?

1 ● ● ● ●
a couple of questions

2 • ● • ●
a couple of questions

3 ● • ● •
a couple of questions

B 🔊 1.15 Put the phrases into the columns. Then listen and check your answers.

at least 50 liters   what sort of coat   a risk of snow
prepare for the worst   I'm sure you know   a good waterproof coat

Pattern 1 • ● • ●   **Pattern 2** ● • • ●   **Pattern 3** • ● ● ●

C Are these statements true or false?

1 Phrases usually have a rhythm where there is a combination of stressed and unstressed words.

2 Words that carry the main meaning, like nouns and verbs, are usually stressed.

3 Functional words, like prepositions and articles, are also usually stressed.

3 SPEAKING SKILLS

A 🔊 **1.13** Look at these sentences from the conversation in exercise 1B on page 16. Find two expressions that indicate danger (D), and two expressions that indicate essential information (E). Write *D* or *E*. Which words in these sentences are unstressed? Listen again to check.

Asking for information

Is there any danger of really bad weather?

What exactly do you mean by "the worst"?

Is there a risk of snow?

What sort of coat **would you recommend** taking?

Providing information

The most important thing to consider is that mountain weather is unpredictable.

First and foremost, you need a good waterproof coat.

One thing to keep in mind is that you don't want a thick coat.

Another thing to consider is the kind of T-shirt you wear.

B ▶ PAIR WORK **Student A: Go to page 157. Student B: Go to page 158. Follow the instructions.**

C Imagine you are going hiking somewhere in the mountains. What two pieces of information would you like to ask for? What information would you give someone going hiking somewhere near you? Use expressions from exercise 3A.

4 PRONUNCIATION: Saying /w/ and /v/

A 🔊 **1.16** Listen to the /w/ sound in these words and then repeat the words.

<u>w</u>eather	<u>w</u>ear	<u>w</u>aterproof	<u>w</u>orst	<u>w</u>ould
q<u>u</u>ick	q<u>u</u>ite	s<u>w</u>im	lang<u>u</u>age	

B 🔊 **1.17** Listen and ⭕circle the word you hear twice. Then check and repeat the words.

1 wet   vet
2 vine   wine

3 worse   verse
4 vest   west

C <u>Underline</u> the /w/ and /v/ sounds in the questions below. Then work in pairs and ask one another the questions.

1 What's the worst weather you've experienced?
2 What would you wear if you were going hiking in winter?
3 Have you ever been worried about your safety?
4 What makes people do very dangerous or weird sports?

5 SPEAKING

A Think of a free-time activity you enjoy. Imagine you're going to give some advice to someone who'd like to take up the activity. What important information could you provide?

B PAIR WORK **Give the advice to a partner. Answer your partner's questions. Then change roles.**

What sort of equipment **would you recommend buying?**

Well, **first and foremost**, you need ...

EXTREME LIVING

1 READING

A   Look at the picture. What do you think would be the most difficult thing about living in this place?
Read the article. Did Noah Harris mention your idea?

❄ COLDER THAN COLD
by Piper Reid

Noah Harris is usually behind the camera, filming documentaries in unusual places. But last month, he took some time out to talk about his most recent – and most extreme – trip. He spent a month at a research center in one of the coldest places on Earth, Antarctica.

First and foremost, I have to ask the question everyone wants to know. How cold was it?

It was absolutely freezing! Where I was, the average temperature was –5°C in January, the warmest month, and –28°C in August, one of the coldest months. I was there in October, and it was about –15°C during the day.

How about the climate in general? What was the weather like, besides cold?

They say Antarctica is the driest, windiest, and brightest continent. It's dry because it's a desert, and surprisingly, it doesn't snow a lot. The area only gets 60 to 80 millimeters of snow a year, but the wind blows up to 185 kilometers per hour. It's full of snow and ice, and everything turns white. But many days there are blue skies and sunshine. It can actually be more difficult to see when the sun is bright.

I am also wondering about the temperature indoors. Where does everyone stay? Is it warm?

I stayed at one of New Zealand's research centers, and all of the buildings are heated. It's one of the 37 centers in Antarctica open all year. In fact, 4,000 people live in Antarctica in the summer months, but only about 1,000 stay for the winter. Where I visited, up to 85 people are at the research center in the warmer months. Fewer people are there when it's colder – about 25. When it's less crowded, everyone has their own bedroom, but when more people are there, it's four to a room.

I am curious about living so close to the same few people in such limited space. What is it like? Does everyone get along?

I was only there for a month – imagine a year of living and working with the same 20 people every single minute of every single day! But everyone really got along well, and they all seem very happy. They have to have good attitudes to survive, but they also love what they do. They're doing some of the most incredible land and ocean exploration in the world.

How was the food? Always an important question!

Eating was the least difficult part of my stay. The chef was totally amazing. People often wanted her to cook meals from New Zealand rather than having international dishes. When you live in an extreme environment, it's nice to have the comforts of home sometimes.

You didn't mention eating local food. What about the fish?

It's against the law to kill any animals in Antarctica. It's also illegal to bring plant life there, so they don't grow food at the research center. All of the food comes by boat or plane. You can't "eat local" in Antarctica!

Final question: What is the most extreme part of living in Antarctica, the biggest challenge?

The scientists often go on trips far from the center to study plant and animal life. Sometimes they camp for up to 100 days! I went on a three-day research trip with a team. After staying in a tent and having no running water or indoor bathroom, the research center seemed like a five-star hotel when I got back!

B   [PAIR WORK]   What are Noah's main points about the weather in Antarctica? The people? The food? What do you think about his experience? Could you live there for a month?

C **UNDERSTAND NUMERICAL WORDS AND PHRASES** Look at the meanings of some expressions with numbers. Find examples in the article. Then think of other things to describe with the expressions.

about = approximately, could be a few more or a few less

average = usual

to = shows a range, the number can fall anywhere in that range

up to = no more than

D **THINK CRITICALLY** In what kind of text would you expect to see a lot of numbers? What kind of information do they provide?

2 WRITING

A Read the description of a town in Canada. What are the town's attractions?

• • • ‹ ›

Drumheller in Alberta, Canada

Drumheller is a town of about 8,000 people in southern Alberta. It's 138 kilometers northeast of Calgary and is located in a desert-like environment. The highest rainfall it gets is about 60 millimeters in June. Temperatures can be extreme. The record highest was 40.6°C, and the lowest was –43.9°C, but the normal range is –18° to 26°C.

Drumheller seems like the least likely place to visit, but almost 500,000 tourists arrive every year. This is because it's the Dinosaur Capital of the World. The Royal Tyrrell Museum has one of the world's largest collections of dinosaur fossils, including more than 200 complete skeletons.

For nature lovers, however, the landscape is even more attractive than the dinosaurs. Parts of it look as strange and dry as the moon's surface, but many species of wildlife live there. The hoodoos are the most fascinating things to see. They're natural towers of rock, up to 6 meters high, with "caps" on the top. People love taking selfies with them.

GLOSSARY

fossil (*n*) part of an animal or plant from thousands of year ago, preserved in rock

B **USE NUMERICAL WORDS AND PHRASES** Complete the phrases with numbers from the description in exercise 2A. Which ones are about distance (*D*), height (*H*), quantities (*Q*), or temperatures (*T*)?

1 a town of about _____ people

2 _____ kilometers northeast of Calgary

3 the record highest temperature was _____

4 the normal temperature range is _____ to _____

5 almost _____ tourists

6 more than _____ complete skeletons

7 up to _____ meters high

C **PLAN** You are going to write a description of an area. With your partner, talk about an area with an interesting environment or features you know. Describe what makes it interesting. You can check online for ideas. Then look at the description in exercise 2A. Do you need to divide your description into paragraphs? What kind of information could you start and end your description with?

FIND IT

D Write your description of the area you discussed in exercise 2C. Use comparative and superlative structures and numerical words and phrases.

E **PAIR WORK** Read your partner's description. Have you visited the area? Would you like to?

REGISTER CHECK

Make an adjective with a noun + *-like* to show that something is similar to something else.

*It's 138 kilometers northeast of Calgary and is located in a **desert-like** environment.*

*The ground is very dry and **rock-like**.*

This is more common in less formal texts, like personal writing, magazines, and web pages.

25 TIME TO SPEAK
Going wild

A **PREPARE** With a partner, talk about natural places you've been to and any outdoor activities you've done. Discuss how they made you feel.

B Imagine you and your partner work for the Wild Ideas travel agency. You're planning a vacation for your class. What kinds of outdoor vacations might they like? Come up with several different ideas and compare them. Use the questions below to help you.

| Home | News | About | Contact Us | 🔍 |

Questions we ask

Where do you want to go? Mountains? Ocean? …

What do you want to see? Landscapes? Wildlife? …

What do you want to do? Hiking? Biking? Kayaking? …

Where do you want to sleep? In a hotel? In a tent? …

How long do you want to stay? A day? A week? …

For many people, outdoor vacations are way too wild. They're too tough, too long, and too far away. At *Wild Ideas*, we're changing that by listening to our customers. They tell us how wild they want to go, and we design a suitable experience for them.

C Work with another pair and share your ideas. Ask for and give each other advice on how to improve your ideas, and note down any useful advice.

FIND IT

D **DECIDE** With your partner, use the advice from part C to help you choose your best idea and improve it. Include interesting facts with numbers. You can look online if you want.

E **PRESENT** Tell the class about your plan. Use superlatives to make it sound attractive. The class compares plans, considers the points below, and votes for the best one. Why is it the best plan?

has most interesting facts   sounds like the most fun   is not too wild or difficult
is something all would enjoy   your own ideas

 To check your progress, go to page 153.

USEFUL PHRASES

PREPARE

I've been to …

I've been … before.

I've gone … in the past.

I went … once.

It felt absolutely …

It made me feel extremely …

It was the … of my life.

The environment was …

PRESENT

One of the most exciting ideas was …

Another great option was …

But that's not all!

Overall, …

20

UNIT OBJECTIVES

■ talk about personality types
■ talk about things you love or hate
■ make and respond to requests
■ write a personal statement for a job application
■ interview for a full-time position

THE WAY I AM

3

START SPEAKING

A Imagine you were on this ride. Which person's expression would yours be most like? What would you say when you got off the ride?

B What does this picture tell us about the personalities of the people? Do you think their faces reveal their true feelings?

C What situations can you think of that reveal what people are really like? For ideas, watch Wendy's video.

EXPERT SPEAKER

Do you agree with Wendy's ideas?

POWER IN QUIET

1 LANGUAGE IN CONTEXT

A **PAIR WORK** **Look at the picture. Which person are you most like? Would you describe yourself as an outgoing person? Why or why not?**

B 🔊 **1.18** **Read and listen to part of a radio show. What are the three personality types mentioned?**

🔊 **1.18 Audio script**

Welcome to *Book Ends*. It's Saturday morning, when we discuss my choice of the week. Today, it's Susan Cain's book titled *Quiet: The Power of Introverts in a World That Can't Stop Talking*, as well as ideas on her website called Quiet Revolution. Cain, whose work explores the character of introverts, feels that American society often prefers extroverts. Her goal is to show that there is power in quiet. She says, "I prefer listening to talking, reading to **socializing**, and cozy chats to group settings. I like to think before I **speak (softly)**." She feels you don't have to **be an extrovert** to be heard.

We often talk about extroverts and introverts, but what do we really mean by these words? An extrovert is someone who easily **attracts attention**, **enjoys the company of** others, and can **be the life of the party**. Some think that extroverts like to **show off**, whereas an introvert is someone who **is reserved**, may find it difficult to **speak up** and express opinions, and often **feels left out** in social situations. These are the two stereotypes accepted by most people, but there's a third personality type, which Quiet Revolution explores: an ambivert. This is a person who sometimes needs quiet and gets energy from it and at other times works best **interacting with people**. I'd never heard of an ambivert before but immediately realized I am one! Which means part of me **is an introvert**. And suddenly, the book got a whole lot more interesting.

GLOSSARY
stereotype (*n*) a set idea that people have about what someone or something is like

C 🔊 **1.18** **THINK CRITICALLY** **Listen and read again. What is the aim of Susan Cain's work? Why do you think she started this project? Do you think it will be helpful to people?**

2 VOCABULARY: Describing personality

FIND IT

A 🔊 **1.19** **Look at the expressions in bold in the script in exercise 1B. Which describe introvert behavior? Which describe extrovert behavior? Can any of the expressions describe both? Define each expression using other words. Use a dictionary or your phone to help you. Listen and check your work.**

B ▶ **Now go to page 142. Do the vocabulary exercises for 3.1.**

C **PAIR WORK** **THINK CRITICALLY** **In what jobs or other areas of life do you think it's helpful to be an introvert? An extrovert? Explain why.**

3 GRAMMAR: Relative pronouns; reduced relative clauses

A Read the sentences in the grammar box. Circle the correct options to complete the rules.

> ### Relative clauses
>
> It's Saturday morning, **when we discuss my choice of the week**.
>
> Cain, **whose work explores the character of introverts**, feels that American society often prefers extroverts.
>
> An extrovert is someone **who easily attracts attention**.
>
> These are the two stereotypes **accepted by most people.** (= that are accepted).

> **!** Use *which* with times, dates, and days when the word defined by the relative clause is a subject or object, **not** a time adverbial.
>
> *She loves **Fridays, which** is the worst day of the week for me.*

1 The relative pronoun can be **the subject** / **the subject or the object** of a relative clause.

2 Use *when* / *which* to add information about particular times, dates, and days.

3 In relative clauses, *who* / *whose* shows possession.

4 Reduced relative clauses **include** / **don't include** the relative pronoun and the verb *be*.

B ▶ **Now go to page 131. Look at the grammar chart and do the grammar exercise for 3.1.**

✓ **ACCURACY** CHECK

Use an article or possessive pronoun with a singular noun followed by reduced relative clauses with *-ed*.

Cain wrote about young introverts ~~in book~~ called Quiet Power. ✗
Cain wrote about young introverts in a/ the/her book called Quiet Power. ✓

C Make true sentences about yourself using relative clauses and the prompts below. Check your accuracy. Then share with a partner. Were any of your ideas similar?

1 going to parties with a lot of people

2 the kind of people you like to be friends with

3 something you like to do in a certain type of weather

4 something you read recently

5 something to describe one of the jobs you've had

4 SPEAKING

A PAIR WORK THINK CRITICALLY Student A: Talk about advantages of being an introvert. Student B: Talk about advantages of being an extrovert. Then try to convince your partner that you're right. Change roles and repeat. Then say which you agree with more.

People **who are introverts** often make good choices. They think about things carefully, which helps them make good decisions.

People **that are extroverts** often **speak up** at meetings and **attract** the boss's **attention**. In the office where I work, people **whose voices are heard** are promoted faster.

3.2 THINGS AND EMOTIONS

LESSON OBJECTIVE
- talk about things you love or hate

1 LANGUAGE IN CONTEXT

A Look at the pictures and identify the objects in them. What do you think of when you see these things? Then read the posts. What is each post about?

Comments

Profile   Sign Out

@dougj: I'm just sitting here, thinking about the strange things I love and hate. For example, most people think crows are **creepy**, but I think they're **impressive**. A crow flying slowly across the sky looks **stunning**. Some people like to stand on beaches, watching sunsets. But I watch big black birds flying by. What about you?

@dannys22: I find mushrooms **disgusting**. Not the taste. It's because they feel like rubber in my mouth. Gross!

> **INSIDER ENGLISH**
>
> *gross* = something extremely unpleasant
>
> *Gross!*   *That's **gross**!*
> *Mushrooms are **gross**.*

@asans5: I love opening a jar of peanut butter and hearing that popping sound! It's more enjoyable than *eating* the peanut butter.

@davidortiz: Popping bubble wrap. It's *so* **satisfying**.

@happyjia: I can't stand touching wool. I find the feel of it really **irritating**. Just looking at it makes me feel **uneasy** and **tense**.

@mandymandy: This might be **bizarre**, but I think the smell of subway stations is **fabulous**. I hardly ever go on the subway these days, but as a child living in New York City, I took it a lot with my mom. Now, that smell reminds me of my childhood.

@greatj: The smell of a swimming pool reminds me of my childhood. I just love it!

@msalex5: I kind of like the smell of gasoline. It reminds me of trips with my family. Maybe we're all a little **weird**!

B Read the posts again. What does each person like or dislike?

C [GROUP WORK] What little things in life do you love and hate?

24

2 VOCABULARY: Strong feelings

A 🔊 **1.20** Look at the words in the box. Cover the posts in exercise 1A on page 24 and look at the pictures. Can you remember which words were used to describe them? Which ones are used to talk about things that are good, bad, or unusual? Listen and check your work.

| bizarre | creepy | disgusting | fabulous | impressive | irritating |
| satisfying | stunning | tense | uneasy | weird | |

B ▶ **Now go to page 143. Do the vocabulary exercises for 3.2.**

EXPERT SPEAKER

C PAIR WORK Describe something that gives you one of the feelings in exercise 2A. Your partner guesses the feeling. Take turns. For ideas, watch Wendy's video.

Do the things that Wendy talks about make you feel the same way? Talk about other things that give you those feelings.

3 GRAMMAR: Present participles

A Read the sentences in the grammar box. Complete the rules.

> **Present participles**
>
> I'm just sitting here, **thinking** about the strange things I love and hate.
>
> A crow **flying** slowly across the sky looks stunning.
>
> Some people like to stand on beaches, **watching** sunsets.
>
> … as a child **living** in New York City, I took it a lot with my mom.

1 To describe two events happening at **the same time** / **different times**, put the verb that describes the second event after a comma, and use the *-ing* form of the verb.

2 To add more information about a **noun** / **verb**, use the *-ing* form of the verb.

B ▶ **Now go to page 132. Look at the grammar chart and do the grammar exercise for 3.2.**

C Look at the present participles in the grammar box in exercise 3A. Make new sentences true for you, using the participles to describe two events happening at the same time or to give more information about a noun.

4 SPEAKING

A PAIR WORK Look at the pictures. How do you feel about these things? Think what you might be doing, seeing, or experiencing when you see these things.

> I think freshly ground coffee smells **fabulous**. It's so nice to smell it, **relaxing** on the balcony every morning.

3.3 ASKING FOR FAVORS

1 LISTENING

A How do you react when your boss or teacher asks you to do something you're not confident about?

B ◀)) **1.21** Listen to the conversation. Kelly is an intern at the International Student Services office of a college. What is she asked to do? What is she worried about? What does her boss, Sandra, suggest?

> **GLOSSARY**
> **intern** (*n*) a student, or someone who has recently finished their studies, who works for a company for a short time, sometimes without being paid, in order to get work experience

C ◀)) **1.22** Listen to Mateo and his boss, David. What is Mateo asked to do? What excuses does he make? What happens in the end?

> **GLOSSARY**
> **deadline** (*n*) a time or day by which something must be done

D ◀)) **1.21 and 22** **LISTEN FOR INFERENCE** Listen to both conversations again. What does Kelly say to show that she's not comfortable talking about the program? What does Mateo say to show he's not happy about giving a presentation?

E **PAIR WORK** **THINK CRITICALLY** We can often guess how people feel, even if they don't say it directly. Discuss the speakers' situations and complete the sentences together. What clues or knowledge do you use to guess how people feel?

1 Sandra probably understands that Kelly is uneasy because _____ .

2 Hwan is probably happy to help because _____ .

3 David wants Mateo to say yes. Therefore, David _____ .

4 Mateo probably feels uncomfortable saying no to David because _____ .

F Do you think Mateo acts professionally with his boss? Why or why not?

2 PRONUNCIATION: Listening for /t/ at the ends of words

A ◀)) **1.23** Listen to the /t/ sounds in this sentence. Which ones are pronounced differently?

I just want the rest of the team to get a general sense of the project.

B ◀)) **1.24** <u>Underline</u> the /t/ sounds in the conversation. Which ones could be pronounced differently? Listen and check.

A That's OK. I just want the rest of the team to get a general sense of the project.

B Um … Sorry, but I wouldn't be comfortable speaking in front of the whole team. My English isn't very good for that kind of thing.

A Your English is fine. Don't worry about it. So, will you do it?

B Yes, I can probably manage that.

C (Circle) the correct options to complete the sentences.

When /t/ is at the *beginning / end* of a word and the sound before it is /n/ or *a vowel / another consonant*, then the /t/ may be pronounced silently. But if that /t/ is also followed by a *vowel / consonant* sound, it might be pronounced more like /d/.

3 SPEAKING SKILLS

A Look at the expressions from the conversations in exercises 1B and 1C on page 26. Write *M* (making a request), *A* (accepting a request), or *R* (refusing a request) next to each one.

Make and respond to requests

1 Is there any chance you could … ?
2 I don't mean to be rude, but …
3 Would you be willing to … ?
4 I'd be happy to help out.
5 Do you think it would be possible (for you) to … ?
6 I don't know how much I'd be able to …
7 Sorry, but I wouldn't be comfortable [-*ing* verb] …
8 Yes, I can probably manage that.

B PAIR WORK With your partner, take turns making and responding to requests in the two situations below. Use expressions from exercise 3A.

1 You need help with an essay.
2 You would like your partner to work next weekend.

C ▶ PAIR WORK Student A: Go to page 157. Student B: Go to page 158. Follow the instructions.

4 PRONUNCIATION: Using polite intonation for requests

A 🔊 **1.25** Listen to each request said twice. Which version sounds more polite to you – the first or the second?

1 Is there any chance you could finish the presentation today?
2 Do you think it would be possible to help me right now?

B 🔊 **1.26** Listen and circle the ending of the request that you think sounds more polite. Then repeat the polite requests.

1 Could you please *think about it?* / *wait for me outside?*
2 Do you think it would be possible for you *to call me back later?* / *to be a little quieter?*
3 Is there any chance you could *speak to her yourself?* / *spell that for me?*
4 Would you be willing to *give the presentation?* / *check my presentation?*

C PAIR WORK Take turns saying these requests to each other politely and agreeing to help. If you think the request is not said politely, try to explain why you feel this way. Then give your partner the chance to try again.

Would you be willing to work on Saturday?

Do you think it would be possible to do that again?

Is there any chance you could come ten minutes earlier?

Would you be willing to share with Alex?

Do you think it would be possible to translate it into English?

5 SPEAKING

A PAIR WORK Role play one of the situations. Decide who makes the request and who responds. The person making the request tries to convince the other to say yes. Then change roles, choose another situation, and repeat.

1 Student A: You want help painting your apartment because you're having a party.
   Student B: You don't like painting.

2 Student A: You need someone to take care of your dog for a week because you're going on vacation.
   Student B: You don't like dogs.

3 Student A: You need someone to give English lessons to your child.
   Student B: You've never worked with children before.

Is there any chance you could take care of my dog for a week, starting this Friday?

Your dog? Um … I don't mean to be rude, but I'm kind of uncomfortable with dogs.

27

3.4 THE RIGHT JOB FOR ME

LESSON OBJECTIVE
- write a personal statement for a job application

1 READING

A Would you like to work with animals? What kind of work would you like to do? What kinds of zoo jobs do you think involve working with animals? Which don't involve working with animals? Read the text. Were any of the jobs you thought of mentioned?

www.wellsbrookzoo/jobs.mzorg

WELLS BROOK ZOO   Job Search • <u>View All Jobs</u> • Internships • Volunteer Opportunities

Are you good with people and penguins? Then the Wells Brook Zoo needs you.

CURRENT JOB OPENINGS

JOB TITLE: Sales Assistant

Position Summary: Sales assistants work in the Wells Brook Zoo gift shop, called Zoovenirs, helping customers with sales.

Responsibilities: You will greet customers as they enter Zoovenirs and answer any questions they may have about the products. You will arrange merchandise, maintaining an organized appearance in the store. You will also be expected to handle cash and credit card sales.

Skills Needed: Experience with customer service and handling cash is preferred. You must have good communication skills and be able to work independently.

JOB TITLE: Zookeeper Assistant

Position Summary: Zookeeper assistants help the zookeepers take care of the animals.

Responsibilities: You will feed a variety of animals, including penguins, birds, and turtles, and will keep animal areas clean and safe. You will enter information into a database about animal behavior and health.

You will also give tours and educational information to school groups visiting the zoo.

Skills Needed: Experience working with animals and speaking in front of people is preferred.

JOB TITLE: Face Painter

Position Summary: Face painters work in areas throughout the zoo, painting animal designs on customers.

Responsibilities: You will paint animals on customers' faces and hands, using a variety of Wells Brook Zoo's preset designs. You will greet customers as they walk by and will take cash and make change if required.

Skills Needed: You must be patient and be able to interact well with children. Previous art training is required, and face painting experience is preferred. You must be comfortable working outside.

JOB TITLE: Assistant Cook

Position Summary: Assistant cooks work in the Wells Brook Zoo cafeteria, helping the cook prepare food.

Responsibilities: You will follow instructions from the head cook as you prepare and cook preset menu items. You will clean kitchen equipment and cookware. You may sometimes have to cook and serve food at food stands located throughout the zoo.

Skills Needed: You must be able to follow instructions but also work independently when necessary. Food service experience is strongly preferred.

Email a personal statement and résumé to wellsbrookzoo.job@mz.org.

GLOSSARY

database (n) information stored in a computer system in an organized way so that it can be searched in different ways
cookware (n) items such as pans, bowls, knives, spoons, etc., used in cooking

B **PAIR WORK** **IDENTIFY AUDIENCE** Read again. Who is the audience for the text? What do you think are the most important responsibilities and skills they need to do and have for each job?

C **GROUP WORK** Which job would you like to have the most? Which job would you be the best at? Give reasons.

D **THINK CRITICALLY** Which aspects of each job are good for introverts? Extroverts? Ambiverts?

2 WRITING

A Read Jonathan's personal statement for the zookeeper assistant job at the Wells Brook Zoo. What are his (1) qualifications, (2) experience, and (3) goals? How good of a candidate do you think he is?

| Jonathan Mendoza | 123 Park Road, Langley, VA 22101 • 575-555-6201 • jmendoza1992@xyz.com |

Personal Statement

I am a recent college graduate with a BS in Animal Science and Management, I have a lifelong interest in animals and birds. Summer jobs as an assistant animal keeper at Rosco Wildlife Center gave me practical experience in observing animals for signs of bad health, preparing their food and sleeping areas, cleaning and repairing their living areas, and educating the public about the inhabitants of the zoo. Interacting with children visiting the zoo was particularly rewarding. I am able to work year-round and on weekends and am excited about helping maintain the excellent standards of animal care at the Wells Brook Zoo. My goals are to expand my knowledge and experience in order to become a full-time zookeeper and to provide the animals with the best environment so that they can enjoy their life in the zoo.

> **REGISTER** CHECK
>
> *In order to* is often used in more formal writing. *To* is often used in less formal writing.
> **Formal**
> *My goal is to expand my experience **in order to** become a zookeeper.*
> **Less formal**
> *My goal is to get more experience **to** become a zookeeper.*

FIND IT

B **PAIR WORK** These are useful words for personal statements: *lifelong interest, expand, maintain, standards.* Find them in the text and discuss what they mean. You can look online for help.

C **COMPOSE AND EVALUATE A PERSONAL STATEMENT** Read the guide to writing and evaluating personal statements. How well does Jonathan's statement follow this advice?

IS YOUR PERSONAL STATEMENT …

CONCISE? Keep it short. Avoid unnecessary words that add no meaning. Avoid overusing the word "I." Vary the sentence structure. Put the information in one paragraph.

RELEVANT? Write about who you are and what you can do. Emphasize only skills and talents relevant to the job. Avoid common expressions such as "good at working on a team" or "a dedicated and enthusiastic worker." Say how you can contribute to the organization. Briefly mention your career goals.

ACCURATE? Check your punctuation (avoid exclamation points), spelling, and grammar.

D **PLAN** You are going to write a personal statement. Work with a partner. Choose one of the other job listings from exercise 1A on page 28. Discuss the skills, experience, qualifications, and goals to include and things to avoid. Then, looking at Jonathan's statement, say how you are going to structure yours.

E Write your personal statement. Then look at the guide in exercise 2C. Have you followed all the tips? Make any changes if necessary.

F **PAIR WORK** **THINK CRITICALLY** Read your partner's personal statement. Which job did they apply for? What are the strongest points in their statement?

TIME TO SPEAK
Getting the job

A **DISCUSS** In many jobs, it's helpful to be good at the things below. In your opinion, what personal qualities do you need in order to do each of them well?

meet deadlines   work on a team   make decisions   give your opinion at meetings

B Work with a partner. Read the text from a company's website. Then imagine you work for this company in human resources. It's your job to interview interns who may have the qualities to become full-time employees. Decide together what to ask in the interviews. Design two or three questions to find out about the things in part A. See the examples below.

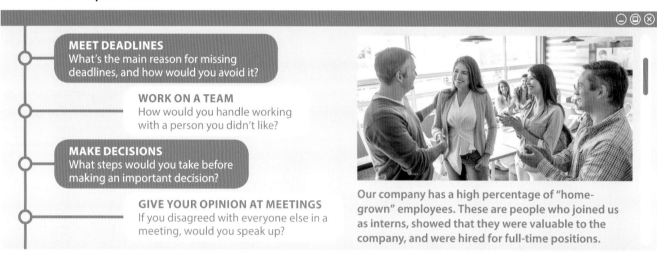

MEET DEADLINES
What's the main reason for missing deadlines, and how would you avoid it?

WORK ON A TEAM
How would you handle working with a person you didn't like?

MAKE DECISIONS
What steps would you take before making an important decision?

GIVE YOUR OPINION AT MEETINGS
If you disagreed with everyone else in a meeting, would you speak up?

Our company has a high percentage of "home-grown" employees. These are people who joined us as interns, showed that they were valuable to the company, and were hired for full-time positions.

C **PREPARE** Work with a different partner. Test your questions from part B. Imagine your partner is an intern and interview them. Change roles and repeat. How well did your questions reveal whether you and your partner have the qualities to work at the company? If necessary, revise your questions to improve them.

D **PRESENT** Tell the class about your questions and why you chose them. The class compares all the questions and chooses the best four. What were the best answers you heard to the four questions?

≫ *To check your progress, go to page 153.* ≫

USEFUL PHRASES

PREPARE

This question revealed that …

Our question about … shows someone who … would be a good employee.

We thought this question would … , but it didn't.

We could improve this question by …

REVIEW 1 (UNITS 1–3)

1 VOCABULARY

A   Complete the paragraph with the correct words.

accept	adapt	company	complex	cope	extrovert
frightened	left	resist	socialize	time-consuming	waste

My family moved to Tokyo, Japan, when I was 17 because of my father's job. I couldn't speak any Japanese, so I was
¹ _____ at first. And Tokyo was so huge and crowded. I had no idea how to ² _____ with so many
changes. I felt ³ _____ out of everything, even though I'm a(n) ⁴ _____ . But then I made some friends
and started to ⁵ _____ again. I also started learning Japanese, which was ⁶ _____ and ⁷ _____ ,
but learning a language is never a(n) ⁸ _____ of time. Anyway, the whole experience taught me that if we don't
⁹ _____ change, but instead ¹⁰ _____ and welcome it, we'll probably ¹¹ _____ to new situations
much better. And for those who enjoy the ¹² _____ of people, it helps to try to make friends right away.

B   PAIR WORK   **Imagine a friend is moving to a different country and is nervous about it. Give them some advice.
Complete the sentences with your own ideas.**

1   It's important to tackle _____ .

2   Don't underestimate your ability to _____ .

3   Try not to be irritated when _____ .

4   Remember: It's never a waste of time to _____ .

5   It's tricky to _____ , but I'm sure you'll be fine.

2 GRAMMAR

A   **Complete the conversation with the correct form of the verbs in parentheses ( ). Use comparative and
superlative forms when necessary. Use *would* and *used to* when possible. Sometimes there is more than one
correct answer.**

A   When I was a kid, I ¹ _____ (hate) vegetables. I ² _____ (not, eat) them but ³ _____ (push)
    them to the side of my plate. I ⁴ _____ (always, cause) trouble at meal times.

B   Well, luckily our tastes in things ⁵ _____ (tend, change) as we get older. In school, I ⁶ _____ (play)
    soccer and basketball, but I ⁷ _____ (never, play) any sports now. My friends say I'm ⁸ _____ (less,
    active) person they know!

A   I'm the opposite. I'm ⁹ _____ (athletic) now than I was before. And what about spending habits? As a child,
    I ¹⁰ _____ (spend) all my money on comics and candy. Now, two of my ¹¹ _____ (big) expenses are
    electronics and my car.

B   For me, a car ¹² _____ (not, useful, enough, spend) money on. It's
    ¹³ _____ (important, see) friends than ¹⁴ _____ (drive) a car.

B   PAIR WORK   **Discuss how your tastes and habits have changed since you were a child.**

3 VOCABULARY

A **Circle the correct options.**

Some people believe that instead of exploring space or the ocean, we should explore our own backyards.
By "backyards," they mean our own local area. They say there are many interesting ¹*species / animal life* in our
local ²*surface / environment*, including rare, ³*endangered / adaptable* ones, that we can discover. So in your area,
there might be a field, a park, a ⁴*sea life / pond*, or a forest where you can ⁵*launch / come across* various birds,
insects, and small animals. It's fascinating to ⁶*explore / observe* these creatures in their natural ⁷*satellite / habitat*.
Backyard ⁸*exploration / origin* can also help teach children why it's important to ⁹*preserve / use up* animal and
plant ¹⁰*life / creature*. It creates a healthy and more pleasant environment for us all. We must learn to live with
the other ¹¹*resources / forms of life* around us. The ¹²*investigation / resources* of our own backyards makes us
appreciate our world.

B **PAIR WORK** **Complete the statements with your own ideas. Then compare ideas with another pair.**

1   I think the idea of exploring our own backyards _____ because
    _____ .

2   I find zoos _____ because the habitat in many of them is
    _____ .

3   It's _____ to monitor animal and plant species because
    _____ .

4   Learning about Earth's resources and forms of life is _____ than learning about
    space because _____ .

5   The most important thing we can do in our lives is _____ . The reason is
    _____ .

4 GRAMMAR

A **Complete the sentences with the correct words.**

considered	found	living	selling	that/which
when	where	which	who	whose

1   In your city, are there any activities _____ encourage people to explore their environment?
2   Describe the area _____ you live.
3   As a person _____ in an urban environment, how do you keep in touch with nature?
4   Do you know any people _____ jobs involve working in nature or with animals?
5   Name someone _____ has helped protect or preserve animal life or natural areas.
6   Name three places _____ to be the most natural and untouched areas in your country.
7   Describe a time _____ you celebrated an occasion outdoors.
8   What are some ways in _____ we can bring nature into our homes?
9   Of all the natural resources _____ in your country, which are the most valuable?
10 Are there any stores _____ green, nature-friendly products near you?

B **PAIR WORK** **Take turns responding to the sentences in exercise 4A. Give as much information as you can.**

UNIT OBJECTIVES

- talk about your support team in life
- make decisions
- discuss advantages and disadvantages
- write a summary
- plan a fund-raising event

COMBINED EFFORT

4

START SPEAKING

A   What are the people doing? Have you or someone you know had a similar experience?

B   What are the benefits of teamwork in this situation? What impact is it having on what the people are doing and how they're feeling?

C   In your opinion, what are the biggest advantages or challenges of teamwork? Discuss your views. For ideas, watch Lucia's video.

EXPERT SPEAKER

Are any of Lucia's ideas different from yours? Do you agree with them?

33

IT TAKES A TEAM

1 LANGUAGE IN CONTEXT

A PAIR WORK Think of people who are important to you. What roles do they have in your life? Then read about eight important kinds of people in our lives. According to the article, which one knows the most about you?

A TEAM FOR LIFE

We all need help sometimes. Most of us have developed a network of "helpers" who play such important roles in our lives that it would be hard to manage without them. Do you recognize any of these people in your life?

The Listener
quietly **keeps an eye on** you and is willing to listen whenever you want to talk.

The Fixer
demonstrates an amazing ability to solve problems. They can suggest practical and creative solutions to problems with technology, the home, your studies, and even relationships.

The Organizer
knows your schedule, wants to **oversee** arrangements, and **acts as** a kind of boss. This helpful person enjoys planning trips, making reservations, buying tickets, and much more.

The Reporter
photographs everything your group does and posts it online. This person helps **build a** good **relationship** in the group by sharing whatever you do together.

The Memorizer
is good at remembering important information. They **take on** the responsibility of reminding you of everything, including what you said and did in the past!

The Teacher
is the one you **turn to** for help, who **assists** you by giving advice about big life decisions. Because of their experience, they can even **steer you away from** trouble.

The Long-Timer
has known you for so long that you've **built** total **trust**. This person knows about your background, experiences, and views. They only need to look at you to know what you're thinking.

The Joker
is always cheerful and makes you laugh. This person **enables you to** see the funny side of life and **contributes** a lot to your happiness.

B Read again. Summarize the main way in which each person is helpful.

2 VOCABULARY: Professional relationships

FIND IT

A 🔊 1.27 Look at the words from the article in exercise 1A in the box. Then describe each one using other words. Use a dictionary or your phone to help you. Listen and check your work.

act as	assist	build a relationship	build trust
contribute	demonstrate	enable (sb) to	keep an eye on
oversee	steer (sb) away from	take on	turn to

B ▶ **Now go to page 143. Do the vocabulary exercises for 4.1.**

C PAIR WORK THINK CRITICALLY Think of a situation for each of the personality types described in the article in exercise 1A in which they would be most helpful. Can you think of any situations where they would do more harm than good? Explain your answers.

3 GRAMMAR: Adding emphasis: *so … that, such … that, even, only*

A   **Read the sentences in the grammar box. Complete the rules with the words in the box.**

> **Adding emphasis: *so … that, such … that, even, only***
>
> … who play **such important roles** in our lives **that** it would be hard to manage without them.
>
> They can **even** steer you away from trouble.
>
> The Long Timer has known you for **so long that** you've built total trust.
>
> They **only** need to look at you to know what you're thinking.

even	only	so	such

1   You can use *so (that)* and *such (that)* to emphasize the result of something. Use _____ + adjective or adverb *(that)*. Use _____ *(an/an)* + (adjective) noun *(that)*.

2   _____ can add emphasis or signal that something is surprising. _____ means "no one else" or "nothing else."

B   ▶ **Now go to page 132. Look at the grammar chart and do the grammar exercise for 4.1.**

C   **Complete the sentences with *so, such, even,* or *only* and your own ideas. Sometimes more than one answer is possible. Then check your accuracy.**

1   Some people have _____ busy lives that …

2   _____ quiet people sometimes want …

3   It's not good to take on _____ much responsibility that …

4   _____ people who know a lot need …

5   Friendship is _____ important that …

D   GROUP WORK   **Compare your sentences from exercise 3C. Whose ideas do you agree with the most?**

> ✔ **ACCURACY** CHECK
>
> **Remember to use a pronoun or a noun after *so* + adjective + *that*.**
>
> *He's so funny ~~that makes~~ everyone laugh.* ✗
>
> *He's so funny that he makes everyone laugh.* ✓

4 SPEAKING

A   PAIR WORK   **Have you ever had to coordinate a group of people? Discuss what the situation was and how it went. How did you feel about being the decision-maker? For ideas, watch Lucia's video.**

EXPERT SPEAKER

Was your experience similar to Lucia's?

I once had to **act as** a guide to a big group of friends who wanted to see my town. It proved to be **such a difficult** task to keep everyone happy **that** I'd think twice before doing it again! I did enjoy being the person they **turned to** for help, though.

35

DESTRUCTIVE TEAMS

1 LANGUAGE IN CONTEXT

A How do you feel when someone criticizes your ideas? Do you think negative comments are useful?

B 🔊 **1.28** Read and listen to an interview with management consultant Zack Sanchez from a podcast called *Better Teamwork*. What are red teams? Sum them up in one sentence.

🔊 **1.28 Audio script**

Host	Every business school graduate knows that good teams are **constructive**, right? Well, Zack Sanchez is here to present another idea: a *destructive* team, or a red team. Zack, welcome to the show.
Zack	Thanks for having me.
Host	So, a red team. What is that exactly?
Zack	Well, first, imagine you're part of a group that's starting a big project. Everyone's excited and congratulating themselves on how great it's going to be. Well, that kind of enthusiasm can actually be dangerous. When everyone is super positive, they often can't see the negative **aspects** of a plan.
Host	I see. So that's why you need a red team?
Zack	Exactly. A red team is two or three people from the group whose job is to play the bad guy – look for **weaknesses** and **draw attention to** possible negative **consequences**. A red team doesn't **weigh the pros and cons**, balancing **strengths** and weaknesses. That's a job for others to do. A red team honestly **assesses** a project and **points out** problem areas.
Host	And teams are open to this? I mean, teams are used to supporting one another, not criticizing each other. I've been on a red team myself, and it wasn't much fun.
Zack	That's why a red team's criticisms should not be **unreasonable**. You've seen for yourself that they need to be **valid** points that have been **thought through** carefully. The other team can't do that by itself.
Host	And that's when destructive becomes constructive.

The red team

C 🔊 **1.28** Read and listen again. What does it mean to "play the bad guy"? How does this relate to red teams?

2 VOCABULARY: Assessing ideas

A 🔊 **1.29** Look at the words from the podcast in the box. Which are verbs / verb phrases? Which are adjectives? Which are nouns? Listen and check your work.

aspect	assess	consequence	constructive	destructive
draw attention to	point out	strength	think through	unreasonable
valid	weakness	weigh the pros and cons		

B ▶ Now go to page 144. Do the vocabulary exercises for 4.2.

C PAIR WORK THINK CRITICALLY Discuss the pros and cons of red teams. Overall, do you think they're a good idea? Would you be a good red team member? Why or why not?

3 GRAMMAR: Reflexive pronouns; pronouns with *other/another*

A **Read the sentences in the grammar boxes. Circle the correct options to complete the rules.**

> **Reflexive pronouns**
>
> Everyone's excited and congratulating **themselves** on how great it's going to be.
> I've been on a red team **myself**, and it wasn't much fun.
> You've seen for **yourself** that they need to be valid points.
> The other team can't do that **by itself**.

1 You can use reflexive pronouns when the subject and object of a sentence are **different / the same**.

2 You **can / can't** use reflexive pronouns to emphasize that an action is performed by the subject.

3 *By* + a reflexive pronoun means **alone, without help / with other people**.

> **Pronouns with *other/another***
>
> Zack Sanchez is here to present **another** idea.   **The other** team can't do that by itself.
> That's a job for **others** to do.
> Teams are used to supporting **one another**, not criticizing **each other**.

4 *Another / The other* is the second half of a pair. *Another / The other* means "one more."

5 *Others* shows there **is one more / are several more** of something.

6 The meaning of *each other* and *one another* is **the same / different**.

B ▷ **Now go to page 133. Look at the grammar chart and do the grammar exercise for 4.2.**

C **Complete the questions with words from the grammar boxes in exercise 3A. Then ask and answer them with a partner.**

1 What sports can people play by _____ ? Do you play any sports by _____ ?

2 What do you and your friends do to enjoy _____ ?

3 Who in your family helps you the most? How do the _____ help you?

4 How can neighbors help each _____ ? In what ways can they annoy one _____ ?

D PAIR WORK **Talk about an experience working on a team. What did the team members do together, and what did they do by themselves? How did they help each other?**

4 SPEAKING

A PAIR WORK THINK CRITICALLY **How do people make group decisions? How effective is this process? What are the challenges?**

In project groups, I find some people want to **draw attention to themselves** and don't listen to others.

And some people just **point out** the **weaknesses** of other people's ideas but don't have any ideas **themselves**.

4.3 TWO PEOPLE, ONE JOB

LESSON OBJECTIVE
- discuss advantages and disadvantages

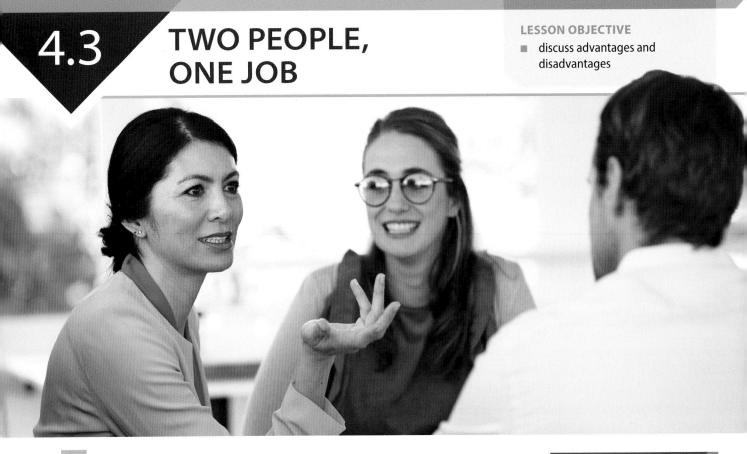

1 LISTENING

A What do you think job sharing is? Have you, or has anyone you know, experienced it?

B 🔊 **1.30** Listen to Rafael and Shelby talk with Heather, their college professor. What advantages and disadvantages of job sharing do they mention?

C 🔊 **1.30** LISTEN FOR ATTITUDE Listen again. Which attitude does each speaker have? Circle one answer for each speaker.

Rafael:	**a** positive	**b** negative	**c** curious
Shelby:	**a** kind	**b** sensible	**c** unreasonable
Heather:	**a** helpful	**b** jealous	**c** unpleasant

D PAIR WORK THINK CRITICALLY Do you think job sharing is a good idea for employees, bosses, and companies? Why or why not?

> **INSIDER ENGLISH**
>
> *be/get stuck with* = be left to deal with something you don't want

2 PRONUNCIATION: Listening for consonant–vowel linking between words

A 🔊 **1.31** Listen to this word group. Which words are linked together, and why?

It's an interesting idea worth considering.

B 🔊 **1.32** Listen. <u>Underline</u> the examples of consonant–vowel linking from exercise 1B.

1 So you're interested in job sharing?

2 I'm interested in finding out more about it.

3 … the advantage of doing the parts of a job you're best at …

4 … that's what I read in an article …

C Circle the correct options to complete the sentence.

When one word finishes in a consonant sound and the next word starts with a *consonant / vowel* sound, the two words are usually linked together when they are in *the same word group / different word groups*.

38

3 SPEAKING SKILLS

A 🔊 **1.30** Look at the expressions from the conversation in exercise 1B on page 38. Are they used to discuss advantages (A) or to discuss disadvantages (D)? Write *A* or *D*. Which words, do you think, might have linked sounds in these sentences? Listen to the conversation again to check.

> **Discuss advantages and disadvantages**
>
> 1 The main benefit is (that) … ____
> 2 A/Another plus is (that) … ____
> 3 The downside is (that) … ____
> 4 One/The tricky issue is (that) … ____
> 5 It gives the company/us/you/me the advantage of [-*ing* verb] … ____
> 6 I'd be / I'm concerned (that) … ____
> 7 The upside is (that) … ____
> 8 One/Another potential problem is (that) … ____

B ▶ PAIR WORK **Student A: Go to page 157. Student B: Go to page 159. Follow the instructions.**

4 PRONUNCIATION: Using stress in compounds

A 🔊 **1.33** Look at these pairs of words. Which word in each pair is stressed? Why?

college student   young children

B 🔊 **1.34** Draw the stress pattern at the top of each column. Then listen and add the phrases to the correct columns.

noun + noun	adjective + noun
college student	young children

C PAIR WORK **Think of some more examples of compounds like these, and use them to make a short story. Give your story to another pair to read out loud. Listen and give them feedback on how they pronounce the compounds.**

5 SPEAKING

A PAIR WORK THINK CRITICALLY Choose a job below or your own idea. Discuss the advantages and disadvantages of job sharing for that job. One person points out the advantages and the other the disadvantages. Then choose another job, change roles, and repeat.

> accountant   chef   dentist
> graphic designer mechanic   receptionist
> teacher   truck driver

It's a good idea for chefs to job share. **The main benefit is** having more personal time for creative projects. And **a plus is** that there are two people to think of ideas for the menu.

I don't know. **One potential problem** is that it can be difficult to agree on the ideas.

THE ME TEAM

1 READING

A **PAIR WORK** Do you prefer working alone or as part of a team? Why?

B **UNDERSTAND AUTHOR'S ATTITUDE** Read the article. Then circle the word in each pair that describes the author's writing.

1 **a** curious   **b** critical
2 **a** objective   **b** subjective
3 **a** optimistic   **b** pessimistic

| HOME | NEWS | BLOG | SIGN IN |

Teamwork makes the dream work?

I'm not so sure.

Bev Shannon
The work-at-home office blogger

We all enjoy being part of a group – there's no better work than teamwork, right? Actually, I disagree. Teamwork can be tough. In fact, it was so difficult that I left my office job and started working from home on my own. It's a much better fit for me, and it has made me think about why teamwork can make our jobs harder rather than easier.

Personalities can make teamwork difficult. There's a famous saying, *There's no "I" in TEAM*, meaning I have to do what's best for the team, not what's best for me. But there's often someone on the team that puts their needs first: "**I** want to do it this way. **My** way is best." The team often goes along with this person, whose ideas might not be the best, just the loudest. Teamwork can be difficult for an introvert, like me. It's hard to speak up if there's a dominant voice in the group. And then there's that team member who likes to argue – and not in a constructive way – who just wants to say "no" because the others said "yes." And, my least favorite, the people pleaser – someone who is such a nice person that they feel they can't be honest. They don't want to hurt anyone's feelings, so they say "yes" to every idea. Just one difficult personality can make teamwork tough. Combine several challenging personality types, and it's even tougher.

Lack of time together can also make teamwork challenging. For example, I was once on a team where we never had enough time to meet as a group. Team member A was at a conference, B had to meet with a customer, C had an important phone call to make, and so on. To successfully work as a team, you need time together – and lots of it.

A final reason teamwork is difficult is because there's often no training on how to work on a team. You can't just put people in a room and expect them to work well with each other. You need to build trust with your team members. Think of football players: They aren't just given a ball and told to play. They practice, and they train. They also have different positions, know who does what, and how they affect one another. It helps to have clear roles on company teams, too, with the right people in them. It's not such a good idea to give the role of a leader to the ME, ME, ME person.

Teams can be tough, but working alone has its challenges, too. When my computer doesn't work, I don't have an IT person to turn to. When I have a great idea, I don't have anyone to share it with to see if it *really is a great idea*. Don't get me wrong – I still like my team of one and enjoy making all of the important decisions myself. But now I realize what was wrong with the teamwork I did in the past and how good teamwork could be if done correctly. And that's useful information – because one day I might want to turn my ME TEAM into a WE TEAM.

C Read again. **What three main reasons does the author give to support her opinion about teamwork? What's her last thought about teamwork?**

D **PAIR WORK** What examples does the author give to support each of her three main reasons? Which do you think are the strongest?

E **GROUP WORK** **THINK CRITICALLY** Think about your answer to exercise C on page 33. Has your opinion changed at all after reading this text? If so, how? Why? What's your attitude toward teamwork?

A Read the summary of an article called "The Power of the Team." Based on the summary, what is the main argument of the article?

●●● < >

In his article "The Power of the Team," Max Jackson states that no one can achieve as much alone as they can on a team. Teamwork is essential to success in personal, educational, and professional situations. The most basic team is the family, which assists and cares for each member in order to make sure the entire family is secure. At school or college, teachers encourage their students to work together in order to produce superior projects or presentations. At work, teamwork is so important that without it, any company would fail. Even healthy competition between teams can build trust and improve relationships within the company. The secret of good teamwork is that each member should contribute their individual skills, talents, and ideas, but never forget that they are working as part of a team toward a common goal.

B **SUMMARIZE MAIN POINTS** A summary is a short version of a longer text. Read about how to write a summary. Then answer these questions about the summary in exercise 2A.

1 What three situations does the writer mention?

2 What are the main points for each situation?

3 Does the last sentence sum up the main points?

REGISTER CHECK

The verb *state* is often used in more formal writing. *Say* is often used in less formal writing.

Summary writing

- Keep your summary short (about ¼ of a page in length). Use one paragraph.
- Use your own words. Don't rewrite the original text.
- Mention the title and author of the text. State the main topic.
- Briefly describe the author's main points.
- After each main point, include the most relevant details or examples.
- Don't add your own opinions. The summary should be based on information from the article.

 WRITE IT

C **PLAN** You're going to write a summary of the article "Teamwork makes the dream work? I'm not so sure." in exercise 1A on page 40. With your partner, look again at the main points and reasons you discussed in exercises 1B and 1C on page 40. Try summarizing them briefly in your own words. Then look at the summary writing tips in exercise 2B and plan the structure of your summary.

D Write your summary of the article.

E **PAIR WORK** **THINK CRITICALLY** Read each other's summaries. What are the strong points of your partner's summary? How do you think you could improve your own summary?

4.5 TIME TO SPEAK
The big event

A **AGREE** Imagine you want to organize a local event to raise money for a cause in your community. Work in a group and choose one of the causes below or think of one of your own.

research at a local hospital   an after-school youth program   improvements to the fire station
new equipment and uniforms for a local sports team   a music program for the local high school

B **DISCUSS** In your group, look at the events below for raising money for the cause you chose in part A. Think of more events. Discuss the advantages and disadvantages of each event. Consider the type of people who would support the cause you chose.

an art show   a barbecue   a concert   a fancy dress party   a marathon   a sports event

C **DECIDE** Choose an event or a combination of events. To help you decide, consider any skills, experience, equipment, or contacts you have that could be useful.

D Think about the jobs your team will need to do before, during, and after the event. Agree on who will be responsible for each job.

E **PRESENT** Tell the class about your event. Explain why it will be popular and why the people on your team have the ability to make it successful. The class chooses the best event.

》》 To check your progress, go to page 154. 》》

USEFUL PHRASES

AGREE
We could try …
Why don't we … ?
That might (not) be the best option …
That could work.

DISCUSS
The main benefit is …
Another plus / potential problem is …
The downside/upside is …
I'd be concerned that …

UNIT OBJECTIVES

- discuss how new technology can help people
- discuss the future of communication
- consider and contrast ideas
- write an online comment with examples
- plan a community improvement project

START SPEAKING

A   **What is happening in the picture? Do you think robots could be better at this activity than humans? Explain your answer.**

B   **Discuss some examples of tasks and situations that a robot might handle better than a human. Say why.**

C   **In your opinion, what things will always be done by humans and never by robots? Why? Discuss some examples. For ideas, watch Carolina's video.**

EXPERT SPEAKER

Do you agree with Carolina's predictions?

1 LANGUAGE IN CONTEXT

A Look at the picture. How does the man feel? How do you feel about flying?

B Read the article about a man's experience with virtual reality. How many times did he use VR therapy? How successful was his experience in the end?

CAN VR THERAPY CURE ME?

I'm scared of flying. Not just a little. Whenever I get on a plane, **I'm scared to death**. I've cried on planes. As an adult. More than once. The fear **isn't rational**, but it is not something **I'm in control of** either. I read about a virtual reality treatment that has helped people like me, so I decided to try it.

STEP 1: GET A REAL THERAPIST
If you want to **try this therapy**, you'll need a therapist. That part's real, not virtual! During my sessions, however, we spent a lot of time in the virtual world. And even then, the therapist was always in control of the software.

STEP 2: PANIC
The first time I put on a VR headset, I was surprised by my body's reaction. When you're in a VR environment, your mind can't tell what's real or not real. Within minutes, I **was panicking**. The therapist taught me how to **regain control** by using **a breathing technique**.

STEP 3: REPEAT
At my first session, my **anxiety level** was extremely high. There was still a lot of fear the second time, but now I **was more conscious of** what was happening. With careful breathing, I **calmed down**. By my third session, I felt almost relaxed.

STEP 4: FLY
Engine noise rising, speed increasing, ground disappearing – and all without the usual fear. I still felt nervous – a real plane is definitely more intense than a VR plane, but I really **had overcome my fear**. VR therapy had worked! I may even take flying lessons if the therapy continues to work so well. Nah!

Adapted from an article by Luke Johnson on the Wareable website

C Read again. What feelings did the man experience before, during, and after the therapy?

2 VOCABULARY: Dealing with emotions

A Look at the expressions in the box. Then describe each one using other words. Use a dictionary or your phone to help you. Then look at how they are used in the article in exercise 1B.

anxiety level	be conscious of	be in control of	**!** *sth* = something
be rational	be scared to death	breathing technique	
calm down	cure (an illness)	overcome my fear	
panic (about sth)	regain control	try a therapy	

B **1.35** Look at the expressions in the box again. Which are verb phrases? Which are noun phrases? Listen and check your work.

C ▶ Now go to page 144. Do the vocabulary exercises for 5.1.

D PAIR WORK THINK CRITICALLY What other strong fears do people have? What advice would you give on how to overcome these fears? Say why.

3 GRAMMAR: Real conditionals

A   **Read the sentences in the grammar box. Which rule is about the *if* clause? Which is about the main clause? Complete the rules.**

> **Real conditionals**
>
> **Whenever** I **get** on a plane, I**'m** scared to death.
>
> **When** you**'re** in a VR environment, your mind **can't tell** what's real or not real.
>
> I **may** even **take** flying lessons **if** the therapy **continues** to work so well.

1 When something is a general fact or a routine, you can replace *if* with *when* and *whenever* in the _____.

2 You can use modals to describe possible future situations and their results in the _____.

B   ▶ **Now go to page 133. Look at the grammar chart and do the grammar exercise for 5.1.**

C   **Write sentences with real conditionals from exercise 3A using the ideas below. Check your accuracy. Then compare with a partner. How similar are your ideas? Ask questions to find out more.**

ask for help	decide to try something new	feel uneasy
see a spider	want to attract attention	

> ✓ **ACCURACY** CHECK
>
> ***Whenever* is one word.**
>
> *I feel scared ~~when ever~~ I'm in a tall building.* ✗
>
> *I feel scared whenever I'm in a tall building.* ✓

4 SPEAKING

A   GROUP WORK THINK CRITICALLY **How can VR be useful in medicine? In sports? For shopping? In training/education? Discuss in your group. For ideas, watch Carolina's video.**

EXPERT SPEAKER

How similar are Carolina's views to yours?

> If someone **wants** to learn how to drive, they **can try** a VR training program first.

> Yeah, I think their **anxiety level won't be** so high **if** they **practice** with an app.

5.2 THE END OF THE OFFICE?

1 LANGUAGE IN CONTEXT

A PAIR WORK In your lifetime, what have been the biggest changes in how we communicate?

B ◀)) 1.36 Read and listen to Ramon and Jack discussing communication in a college debate. Do they change their attitudes in the end?

◀)) 1.36 Audio script

Helena	The topic for this month's debate is the office of the future. We've asked millennials Ramon and Jack if they'd rent traditional office space for a future company or go virtual.
Ramon	Right. Well, millennials will soon be the largest group of workers. We communicate virtually day and night and **have no desire to** work in an office 9 to 5. Millennials will **be eager to** work for a virtual company as long as the technology is good.
Jack	OK, that may be true, but only if we're talking about future workers. Many current employees, older than us, **aren't prepared to** work like that. Even if the tech is amazing, face time is important.
Ramon	But how important? Companies can save hundreds of thousands of dollars a year in rent if they go virtual.
Jack	Well, I'm **not against** saving money, and I'**d be more than happy to** use videoconferencing for most meetings. But if you'**re passionate about** an idea and **are dying to** share it, you want to do it in person. You can't really connect with your team unless you're all in a room together.
Ramon	*All* communication will be virtual eventually, so we shouldn't **be reluctant to** lead the way. It could be the next big thing, providing companies invest more in technology.

GLOSSARY
millennial (*n*) a person who was born in the 1980s, 1990s, or early 2000s
face time (*n*) time spent talking to people directly, not virtually

C ◀)) 1.36 Read and listen again. What does Ramon think about the office of the future? What does Jack think? What reasons do they give? Who do you agree with?

2 VOCABULARY: Willingness and unwillingness

FIND IT

A ◀)) 1.37 Look at the expressions in the box. Which ones were used in the script in exercise 1B? Use your phone to find examples online of the expressions that are not in the script, or make your own sentences. Which expressions mean you want to do something, and which mean you don't want to do something? Listen and check your work.

be against	be anxious to	be dying to	be eager to
be more than happy to	be passionate about	be prepared to	be reluctant to
be unwilling to	have no desire to	have no intention of	hesitate to

B ▶ Now go to page 145. Do the vocabulary exercises for 5.2.

C PAIR WORK Discuss how your friends and family communicate in different situations. When are they eager to talk face-to-face? What ways of communication are they reluctant to use?

3 GRAMMAR: Conditionals: alternatives to *if*

A **Read the sentences in the grammar box. Circle the correct options to complete the rules.**

> ### Conditionals: alternatives to *if*
>
> Millennials will be eager to work for a virtual company **as long as** the technology is good.
>
> That may be true, but **only if** we're talking about future workers.
>
> It could be the next big thing, **providing** companies invest more in technology.
>
> **Even if** the tech is amazing, face time is important.
>
> You can't really connect with your team **unless** you're all in a room together.

> **!** *Providing* and *as long as* are more common in writing.

1 Use *as/so long as*, *only if*, and *providing/provided* to show that the result **will / won't** happen when a specific condition becomes true.

2 Use *even if* when you believe the result **will / won't** change. *Even if* means "whether or not."

3 Use *unless* to describe a possible **positive / negative** condition in the present or future. It has a similar meaning to "except if" or "if … not."

B ▶ **Now go to page 134. Look at the grammar chart and do the grammar exercise for 5.2.**

C PAIR WORK **Complete the sentences with your own ideas. Then compare and discuss your ideas with a partner.**

1 Even if virtual reality improves a lot, _____ .

2 I wouldn't want to _____ unless I was paid a lot of money.

3 I'm prepared to work long hours, providing that _____ .

4 As long as _____ , I feel comfortable with people.

5 I'm more than happy to work in an office, but only if _____ .

4 SPEAKING

A GROUP WORK THINK CRITICALLY **How, and under what conditions, can changes in technology affect the way we communicate with these people?**

bank staff   coaches / gym staff   doctors/therapists   government employees   teachers

> I think we'll have more doctor's appointments by video call, **providing** our privacy is protected.

> Yeah, but **only if** people are prepared to accept that. Some people **are unwilling to** share private information virtually.

5.3 STOP BLAMING GAMING

1 LISTENING

A 🔊 **1.38** Talk about some good and bad things people say about video games. Then listen to a TV debate about video gaming. How many of your ideas do the speakers mention?

GLOSSARY
isolation (*n*) being alone, especially when this makes you feel unhappy

B 🔊 **1.38** Listen again. What does Parker think is a problem? Why does Nadia think gaming is a social activity?

C 🔊 **1.38** **LISTEN FOR SPEAKER'S DEGREE OF CERTAINTY** Listen again. Is the speaker certain or uncertain about their ideas? Listen to the language around these ideas and check (✓) the ones that sound confident.

1 ☐ **Parker**: If you can't control your gaming, it's a problem.
2 ☐ **Host:** Young people spend 20 hours a week gaming.
3 ☐ **Parker:** A lot of people spend too many hours gaming.
4 ☐ **Nadia**: We would hear about major problems with gaming if there were any.
5 ☐ **Nadia**: Gaming doesn't cause isolation. It's a social activity.

D **PAIR WORK** **THINK CRITICALLY** Whose views on video games seem the most believable? Why? Which view do you agree with?

2 PRONUNCIATION: Listening for lower pitch information

A 🔊 **1.39** Listen to this sentence. How are the underlined phrases connected to the noun phrases before them? What do you notice about how they are pronounced?

With me to discuss this is Nadia Rivera, <u>a video game developer</u>, and Parker Wendell, <u>from the group Game On – Game Off</u>, which offers advice about gaming.

B 🔊 **1.40** Listen to the sentence and then to a version of it with extra information added in parentheses. Repeat the original sentence and then the new version.

And it's fantastic for the brain. It improves thinking speed, the ability to concentrate, and problem-solving skills.

And it's fantastic for the brain. It improves thinking speed (information processing), the ability to concentrate (how long we can concentrate for), and problem-solving skills (like critical thinking).

C (Circle) the correct options to complete the sentence.

When extra information is added next to a noun phrase, for example to define, explain, or give more details about the noun phrase, this extra information is usually pronounced *as part of the same / with a different* tone in a *lower / higher* key.

3 SPEAKING SKILLS

A Look at the expressions from the TV program in exercise 1A on page 48. Which ones show the speaker is certain, uncertain, or giving a contrasting idea? Complete the chart.

> At the same time, …
> It's a well-known fact (that) …
> Who knows …
>
> I don't have a clue …
> On the contrary, …
> You can bet (that) …
>
> I guarantee (that) …
> That said, …

Certain	Uncertain	Giving a contrasting idea

B Find the best place in the sentences below to add one of the expressions from exercise 3A. Use a different expression in each sentence. Then tell a partner if you agree with the statements. Say why or why not.

1 Most children like playing video games.

2 Video games are not relaxing. They're stressful.

3 VR games are the future, but there will soon be something even better.

4 … what crazy video games creators will come up with ten years from now.

5 Many games help develop useful skills and should be encouraged. We have to be careful about the time we spend playing them.

C ▶ PAIR WORK Student A: Go to page 157. Student B: Go to page 159. Follow the instructions.

4 PRONUNCIATION: Saying front vowels /ɪ/, /e/, and /æ/

A ◀)) 1.41 Listen. Then repeat the words and focus on the underlined vowels.

/ɪ/	vi̱deo	fi̱gures	li̱sten	i̱ndustry	bi̱llion
/e/	te̱n	ple̱asure	be̱t	sa̱id	fri̱ends
/æ/	a̱verage	a̱sk	fa̱ntastic	exa̱ct	a̱ctually

B Circle the correct options to complete the sentences.

The tip of the tongue is nearer to the *front / back* of the mouth for these vowels. The jaw moves *down / up* as you go from /ɪ/ to /e/ to /æ/.

C ◀)) 1.42 Listen and circle the words you hear.

1 bit bet bat

2 slipped slept slapped

3 tin ten tan

4 sit set sat

5 rip rep wrap

6 hid head had

D PAIR WORK Take turns saying one of the words from exercise 4C. Your partner should repeat the word you said.

5 SPEAKING

A PAIR WORK THINK CRITICALLY What are the different ways that video games can benefit people of all ages?

> It's a well-known fact that some video games can improve concentration and reaction speed. At the same time, we have to be conscious of the amount of time spent gaming …

49

5.4 WHAT LANGUAGE BARRIER?

1 READING

A   Have you ever used a translation app? Did you find it useful? Read the article. According to Lance, how can people be helped by translation apps? What can't they do?

👤 Sign up   ▷ Log in

🚲 THE TRAVELER'S TAKE

— By Lance Levine

Do translation apps break down barriers or put up new ones?

A few years ago, while I was on a cycling trip in Brazil, I fell off my bike. I was a little banged up, but the front wheel of my bike was damaged badly. It looked like I was in for a difficult day. I needed tools to fix the bike, and I only had an air pump and some glue. I had seen a house a few minutes before, so I picked up my bike and started walking.

My Portuguese consisted of "please" and "thank you," so the language barrier was an issue. I had no idea how to explain what happened or ask for help or a ride to town. Then I remembered my translation app! What a relief. I spent about 20 minutes on the side of the road tapping out the story and creating requests for different things. I knew it wouldn't be perfect, but at least it would tell people the basics. I approached the house, app in hand, and knocked on the door.

Before I could press PLAY on my carefully constructed greeting, the elderly woman who answered the door was on the job. One look at me, my damaged bicycle, my dirty knees and torn shirt, and that translation app was about as useful as air conditioning on a motorcycle.

In five minutes' time, I was sitting on the patio with my leg on a stool, clean and bandaged. Maria (the elderly woman), her husband Gustavo, two of their kids, seven of their grandchildren, and a constantly changing group of neighbors had appeared from nowhere, and my tragedy was quickly becoming a party. Gustavo and a neighbor were enjoying a heated debate about the best way to repair the wheel on my bicycle. The kids were exploring the contents of my backpack piece by piece and finding each hilariously funny. And the smell of food started to fill the air. A bike accident is usually a bad thing. But by the time Maria and her son João left me at my hotel that night, with a full stomach and a shiny, clean, fully repaired bicycle, I felt like the luckiest man in the world.

We're so independent these days. The internet and smartphones make information and services so easy to access. Translation apps, too, have their place and are very useful. I think from now on, though, I'm going to use that app for work or maybe in stores when I travel and need something specific. When it comes to people, I'll take the risk.

I won't catch story details, and I'll misunderstand instructions now and again. I'll definitely have trouble with jokes, but humor usually doesn't translate, even if your app gives you all the right words. I'll get surprises, maybe some bad ones but mostly good ones. I'll get to act things out and look ridiculous doing it, and I'll get to solve the puzzle of what someone else is trying to tell me. I'll get gestures, laughter, attention, and the kindness of strangers.

Language barrier? What language barrier?

GLOSSARY
barrier (*n*) something that prevents communication, action, or progress
gesture (*n*) a movement you make with your hand, arm, or head to express your meaning

B   **UNDERSTAND PROBLEMS AND SOLUTIONS** Read again. After his crash, what problems did Lance expect to have? What happened instead?

C   What's Lance's opinion of translation apps?

D   **PAIR WORK** **THINK CRITICALLY** What's your opinion of translation apps? Do they make it harder to show our feelings, or do they enable us to have conversations we never thought possible?

INSIDER ENGLISH

Be in for means *be about to experience something unpleasant.*

2 WRITING

A Read Julieta's comment in response to Lance's article in exercise 1A on page 50. What's her opinion of translation apps? How many situations does she describe to support her opinion?

COMMENTS

Julieta M.
New York

I think translation apps are great, but I use them more for writing than speaking. My company does business with an Italian company. We usually communicate in English, but sometimes they send me information in Italian. My app translates them just fine. I also exchange emails with a Chilean friend. Her English is only beginner level, so I use my app to send her messages in Spanish and to translate her messages. OK, we could try English, but I think she'd gradually stop writing. As long as I use my app, everything's fine.

As for speaking, when I was in Tokyo once, I got lost on my way to a meeting. I just stood there on the street, helpless. Finally, I stopped a man and used my app to ask, "Excuse me. Where's the Panorama Building?" He looked surprised, so I played it again. Then he laughed and pointed at the building right behind me. Well, at least I didn't have far to walk! So yes, I'm a big fan of these apps.

💬 2   ♡ 7   ⇄ 1

REGISTER CHECK

We use different organizing and connecting expressions in informal and formal texts. Look at these formal examples. Find informal examples in Julieta's comment.

Formal

That said, we could try English.

With regards to speaking, when I was in Tokyo once …

Therefore, I'm a big fan of these apps.

B **STATE OPINION AND GIVE EXAMPLES** Read about one way to organize an opinion comment. Then check Julieta's comment in exercise 2A. Does it have all these features?

1 **Make an opening statement.** Give your opinion of translation apps: for, against, or mixed feelings.

2 **Support your opinion with examples.** For each example, …
   - **give some background.** Give a short explanation about the situation at the beginning.
   - **describe what happened.** You can include direct speech if you want.
   - **add a comment.** You can comment after each example, e.g., *My app translates them just fine.*

3 **Make a closing statement.** Give your opinion again but in different words.

 WRITE IT

C **PLAN** You are going to write a comment in response to Lance's article. With a partner, discuss your opinion and give examples. The examples can be about your own or other's experiences. Then plan your opening statement, background information, description of what happened, and your closing statement.

D Write your comment.

E **PAIR WORK** Exchange your comments with a different partner. Do you have the same opinion about translation apps? What do you think about the examples your partner gave?

TIME TO SPEAK
Community improvement campaign

FIND IT

A Talk about a community project or event you know about. What was its purpose? Did it involve working with technology? How successful was it? Tell a partner. You can look online for ideas if you need to.

B **DECIDE** Work with a group and choose something to improve in your community. Use one of the ideas below or your own idea. Discuss how people will benefit from the project.

clean up and improve a public space   create after-school programs for teens
plan social events or activities for elderly people   start a community garden

C **DISCUSS** With your group, talk about the resources you'll need. How can you use technology in your project? What other materials or tools will you need? What roles will people have? Think of ways to do the project as cheaply as possible and how to encourage others to help.

D **PREPARE** Come up with a plan for your project. Decide how you'll get the resources you talked about in part C.

E **PRESENT** Present your plan to the class. Agree on which plan will benefit the community the most. Which project, other than your own, would you most like to work on?

To check your progress, go to page 154.

USEFUL PHRASES

DECIDE
Now that's a good idea.
On second thought, …
That said, …
Good point.
I see what you mean.

DISCUSS
It's a well-known fact that …
At the same time, we need …
You can bet that …
As long as … , we can …

That will work providing (that) …
If … , we'll …
Who will be in control of …

UNIT OBJECTIVES
■ describe unexpected fame
■ talk about unexpected situations
■ make assumptions
■ write an interesting story
■ tell a story

EXPECT THE UNEXPECTED

6

START SPEAKING

A   What is the situation in the picture? Do you think the people expected this situation? How are they reacting? How would you react?

B   Think of some unexpected situations, like winning a lottery or meeting a well-known person. Discuss how you would react in these situations.

C   Describe a time when something totally unexpected happened to you or someone you know. How did you, or the person you know, react? For ideas, watch Bojan's video.

EXPERT SPEAKER

How would you handle the situation Bojan describes?

6.1 GOING VIRAL

Kyle MacDonald

1 LANGUAGE IN CONTEXT

A Look at these pictures. What are they? How do you think they are connected to Kyle MacDonald? Then read the article and check your guesses.

FROM PAPERCLIP TO A HOUSE

What **makes a story entertaining** enough to go viral? In Kyle MacDonald's case, it was a simple red paperclip. He exchanged it online, and then kept trading for better things until he reached his final goal – his own house.

The 26-year-old from Vancouver had been trading things online for a year before he finally got offered a two-story, three-bedroom, 1920s farmhouse in Kipling, Canada, and **made the headlines**. The 14 trades that he made included a fish pen; a stove; an "instant party kit"; a snowmobile; a vacation to Yahk; a moving van; a recording contract; a year's free rent in Phoenix, Arizona; and a part in the movie *Donna on Demand*.

When Kyle was growing up in the suburbs of Vancouver, he watched children go door to door trying to trade their toys for something more valuable. He was sure as long as he tried hard enough, he would get what he wanted. And sure enough, an opportunity presented itself.

Not many people **had heard of** the small town of Kipling before the story **caught people's attention**. The mayor, Pat Jackson, was trying to promote tourism and decided to make the offer of the house to **get publicity** and **raise awareness of** the town as a friendly, welcoming place. His offer included not just the house, but the key to the town and the opportunity to be mayor for one day.

Since the trade Mr. MacDonald has **made an appearance** on a TV show, given interviews to newspapers, and set up a popular website. The red paperclip was definitely his ticket to fame.

Adapted from an article on the Mail Online website

GLOSSARY
trade (*n/v*) exchange one thing for another

FIND IT

B Read again. How did Kyle achieve his goal? Who is the other person in the story? What role did he play?

C [PAIR WORK] Can you think of another example when an ordinary person became accidentally famous? Tell your partner. You can check online if you need to.

2 VOCABULARY: Talking about fame

A ◀) **1.43** [PAIR WORK] Look at the expressions in the box and discuss their meaning. Then listen and check the definitions. Which of them were used in the article? Can you use any of the expressions to talk about the story you told in exercise 1C?

catch sb's attention	do a/the broadcast	get hits	get publicity
have a good/bad reputation	have (never) heard of sth	make an appearance	make sth entertaining
make headlines	praise sb	raise awareness (of sth)	seek fame

B ▶ Now go to page 145. Do the vocabulary exercises for 6.1.

C [PAIR WORK] Why do people seek fame? What are the pros and cons?

D [PAIR WORK] Imagine that your name appeared in the news headlines. What would your reaction be? Tell your partner. For ideas, watch Bojan's video.

EXPERT SPEAKER
Is Bojan's reaction similar to yours?

54

GRAMMAR: Narrative tenses

A **Read the sentences in the grammar box. Complete the rules with the correct tenses below.**

> **Narrative tenses**
>
> The 26-year-old from Vancouver **had been trading** things online for a year before he finally **got offered** a two-story, three-bedroom, 1920s farmhouse.
>
> Not many people **had heard** of the small town of Kipling before the story **caught** people's attention.
>
> The mayor, Pat Jackson, **was trying** to promote tourism and **decided** to make the offer of the house.

> past continuous
> past perfect (*had* + past participle)
> past perfect continuous (*had* + *been* + verb + -*ing*)
> simple past

1 Use the _____ for an ongoing action or situation that continued up to an event or situation in the past.

2 Use the _____ to describe a completed event that happened before another event in the past.

3 Use the _____ for the main completed events or situations in a story. Use the _____ for background activities happening at the same time as the main event.

B ▶ **Now go to page 134. Look at the grammar chart and do the grammar exercise for 6.1.**

C [PAIR WORK] **Read the beginning and end of a story. With a partner, take turns making sentences to complete the story. Use a variety of narrative tenses.**

Matt wanted his marriage proposal to be special, but he never expected it to make headlines …

… This was a truly happy ending.

> Matt wanted his marriage proposal to be special, but he never expected it to **make headlines**. He **had been planning** the speech for months …

> … and **chose** what he thought was the perfect ring …

4 SPEAKING

A ▶ [PAIR WORK] **Student A: Go to page 158. Student B: Go to page 159. Follow the instructions.**

NOT AGAIN!

1 LANGUAGE IN CONTEXT

A   GROUP WORK   Think of a time when something did not go according to plan for you. What happened? Were you disappointed? Why? What would have made the situation better?

B   ◀》 1.44   Read and listen to the podcast. What was disappointing about each situation? What do you understand by "managing expectations"?

◀》 1.44 Audio script

Mike   Accidents happen. Things outside our control can go wrong. So how can we make sure we keep our promises?

Tessa   And keep people around us happy?

Mike   Exactly. Managing expectations might be the key. It may be that explaining things clearly, promising less, and delivering more is all it takes. Let me give you an example of when that didn't happen for me. I was waiting for a flight. The airline **confirmed** that it was on time. A few minutes later, they said it was late. No surprises there. They **estimated** it would be delayed by about 30 minutes. Then they **announced** there could be an even longer wait. And on it went. Each time, they said we wouldn't have to wait much longer … Four hours later we took off. Unbelievably frustrating.

Tessa   Yeah, I totally get it. I have this friend who's always late. She'll **swear** she'll be there at a certain time, and she'll always keep me waiting for ages and doesn't even call or anything. The last time we had plans, I told her I **had doubts about** her being there. She **denied** she'd ever been late and **insisted** she could make it. But guess what! No show. I wish she'd said she might be late and **proposed** a less ambitious time. I would have been so happy to see her waiting for me for a change.

C   ◀》 1.44   THINK CRITICALLY   Read and listen again. For each situation, how could the speakers' expectations have been managed better? In general, what different steps can you take to manage people's expectations?

2 VOCABULARY: Reporting verbs

A   ◀》 1.45   Look at the words and phrases in the box. How many can you find in the podcast? Which ones can you use to complete: (a) Both sentences below? (b) Only sentence 1? (c) Only sentence 2? Which verb doesn't work in either sentence? Listen and check your work. In what situations would you use each of these verbs?

announce	argue	boast	claim	confirm	deny
estimate	have doubts about	hope to	insist	propose	swear

1   He … that the plan would work.   2   He … the plan.

B   ▶   Now go to page 146. Do the vocabulary exercises for 6.2.

C   PAIR WORK   Have you been in a situation similar to the ones described in the podcast in exercise 1B? Tell your partner what happened. Use the words in the box above.

3 GRAMMAR: Reported speech with modal verbs

A **Read the sentences in the grammar box. Complete the rules.**

Reported speech with modal verbs

Direct speech	Reported speech
"It **will be** delayed by about 30 minutes."	They **estimated** (that) it **would be** delayed by about 30 minutes.
"There **could be** an even longer wait."	They **announced** (that) there **could be** an even longer wait.
"You **won't have** to wait much longer."	They **said** (that) we **wouldn't have** to wait much longer.
"I **can make** it."	She … **insisted** she **could make** it.
"I **might/may be** late."	I wish she'd **said** (that) she **might be** late.

In reported speech, change *will* to _____ . Change *can* to _____ and *may* to _____ .
Other modals like *might*, *should*, and *could* don't change.

B **Now go to page 135. Look at the grammar chart and do the grammar exercise for 6.2.**

C 🔊 **1.46** **PAIR WORK** **Listen to the messages and announcements and make notes. Take turns reporting them to each other. Then check your accuracy. When was the last time you heard similar messages? Do you remember what they said?**

> ✓ **ACCURACY** CHECK
>
> Unlike most other verbs, use an object after *tell* in reported speech.
> *He ~~told~~ that it wouldn't rain in June.* ✗
> *He told me that it wouldn't rain in June.* ✓
> *He said/swore/insisted that it wouldn't rain in June.* ✓

4 SPEAKING

A **PAIR WORK** **Imagine you've heard some news items and you need to report them to someone who'll be affected by them. How will you deliver the news? Use the situations below and your own ideas.**

■ City authority announcement: The new highway won't be ready for another two years because of costs, so your friend who commutes to work could be asked to use the longer route into the city.

■ Soccer club newsletter: The star player of your friend's favorite soccer team has been injured, and the management may not be able to find a replacement in time for an important game.

■ Real estate agent announcement: The construction of the apartment building where your friend bought an apartment has been delayed, they guess by about three years because the builders have discovered archaeological items on the site.

B **PAIR WORK** **THINK CRITICALLY** **Think about the news items from exercise 4A. How can officials in charge manage people's expectations in these situations using strategies you discussed in exercise 1C on page 56?**

SOMETHING IN THE WATER

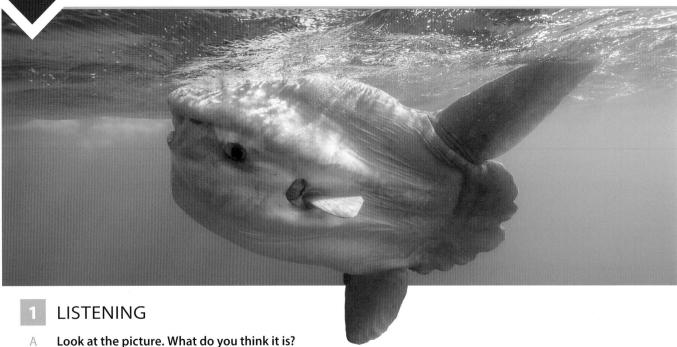

1 LISTENING

A Look at the picture. What do you think it is?

B 🔊 **1.47** Listen to a TV reporter interviewing a couple on the beach. What did they see? How did they react?

C 🔊 **1.47** Listen again. What do Brice and Cynthia remember differently?

D 🔊 **1.48** What do you think happened in the end? Listen to the rest of the report and check. Was your prediction correct?

E 🔊 **1.49** **UNDERSTAND MEANING FROM CONTEXT** Listen to the entire report. What do *fin*, *shaken*, and *narrow escape* mean? What other words helped you figure out the meaning?

F **PAIR WORK** **THINK CRITICALLY** Compare the reporter's assumptions about what happened with Brice's and Cynthia's stories. Which assumptions were totally correct, partly correct, or incorrect?

2 PRONUNCIATION: Listening for complex verb phrases

A 🔊 **1.50** Listen and complete the sentences. Compare with a partner. Which of the missing words are stressed, and which are not stressed?

1 You _____ terrified.

2 I _____ pretty fast myself.

3 And if you _____ never _____ an ocean sunfish …

B 🔊 **1.51** <u>Underline</u> the verb phrases. Read them aloud. Then listen to how they are pronounced on the recording.

I've never seen Brice swim so fast.

It must have been like a scene from *Jaws*.

There may have been some screaming.

It would've been cool to tell people we'd had a narrow escape.

C Circle the correct options to complete the sentence.

When there is a complex verb phrase, the auxiliary verbs are usually *stressed / unstressed* and *contractions / full forms* are often used.

3 SPEAKING SKILLS

A Look at the expressions in the chart. Which ones mean "That's partly true"? Which ones mean "That's not true"? Which two words could be changed to *guess*?

Making assumptions	Contradicting assumptions	Clarifying assumptions
You/It must have been …	Not at all.	Up to a point.
I suppose …	Not in the least.	To an extent.
I assume …	Absolutely not.	In a way.

B PAIR WORK   Imagine your partner was in the water when the sunfish appeared. You're a reporter. Interview your partner, making assumptions about how they felt. Your partner reacts. Use the expressions in exercise 3A. Take turns.

4 PRONUNCIATION: Saying short and long vowels

A 🔊 1.52 Listen to the recording. Can you hear the difference between the first and second word? Repeat the words and focus on the underlined vowels.

/ɪ/ l<u>i</u>st   /i/ l<u>ea</u>st
/ʊ/ f<u>u</u>ll   /u/ f<u>oo</u>l

B 🔊 1.53 Listen and ⟨circle⟩ the first kind of vowels and <u>underline</u> the second kind of vowels.

Sue could see a shark in the sea, so the first thing she did, after screaming, was to reach for her new phone to film it. Sue's phone was deep in her beach bag, and by the time she had found it, sadly, the shark had swum farther away.

C Practice saying the sentences in exercise 4B, paying attention to the short and long vowels.

5 SPEAKING

A PAIR WORK   Choose a situation in the box or your own idea. Student A starts by saying one sentence about the event. Student B asks questions, making assumptions about how Student A felt. Student A reacts. Then Student B chooses a different event, and Student A asks questions.

bus broke down   saw an unusual animal   got lost on a hike or in a city   went to an interesting party

A few weeks ago, I went to an underwater wedding.

I assume you were wearing a diving suit.

B GROUP WORK   Tell your group what your partner in exercise 5A said about the event. Whose story was the most interesting?

YOU MAY EXCHANGE RINGS

GETTING IT WRONG

1 READING

A **PAIR WORK** **Have you ever made an embarrassing mistake? What happened?**

B **Read the posts. Which one is about the wrong gift? The wrong place? The wrong time? Summarize what went wrong in each story in one sentence.**

INSIDER ENGLISH

it hit + object pronoun = just realized something
Then it hit me.
Suddenly, it hit her.

Serena B
102 posts

My dumbest mistake was just recently. My best friend's wedding was in Salt Lake City. My husband and I, who live in Los Angeles, decided to make a long weekend of it. I planned it all out very carefully: Drive to Las Vegas on Friday (six hours) and then drive to Salt Lake City (four hours) the next morning. We'd drive the whole ten hours back on Sunday. And the plan worked! We got to Vegas right on schedule, had a great night out, and were on the road by 10:30 the next morning. The wedding wasn't until 4:00, so we took our time and enjoyed the landscape, which is so beautiful. At 3:40 p.m. we pulled into the (very full) parking lot and went inside to get seats. The place was packed, but no one was seated, which was weird. Then, even weirder, we saw the bride and groom standing around chatting with people. I told my husband I hadn't expected to see them until after the ceremony. Then it hit me. Salt Lake City is an hour ahead of Las Vegas. It wasn't 3:45. It was 4:45, and the wedding was over. What a great job I did of planning that weekend!

👍 Like 💬 Comment

Vicky S
83 posts

My grandmother lived with us when I was a kid, but sometimes she'd go stay with my uncle, who lived about four hours away. They'd all meet at a McDonald's about halfway between them, and grandma would go home with my uncle. The summer I got my license, I decided I'd be grandma's driver. Mom didn't like the idea but finally agreed. She kept repeating the directions and wanted me to write them down, but I reminded her that I could use the GPS. Nothing could possibly go wrong! That was true for about 90 minutes. There was a big detour through a strange town because of road work, but we finally got back on the highway and eventually arrived at McDonald's. When we went inside, there was no sign of my uncle, so we waited. And waited. After a while we called my uncle to check what was taking him so long, and he said he'd been waiting for us for half an hour! Guess what! The GPS had taken us to the wrong McDonald's. Grandma had commented on the different layout, but we just assumed they'd redecorated. All these restaurants and parking lots look so similar. Needless to say, that was the last time I drove grandma anywhere.

👍 Like 💬 Comment

Ivan P
147 posts

I hadn't been living in Marshall long when I met my new friend Jim and his wife Dana. Since I was new in town, I was really happy when Dana invited me to Jim's birthday party. I thought it would be a good way to meet new people. She said that there would be food and even a band. She insisted that I shouldn't bring anything. But I wanted to make a good impression with a nice gift for Jim. I didn't know him well, but I remembered he said he loved baseball. So I got him a Detroit Tigers T-shirt. I thought he probably wore a large. When I got there, I saw animal decorations and realized the party was for *little Jim*, Dana and Jim's one-year-old son. I suppose little Jim liked his new large T-shirt as much as I liked listening to *The Happy Journey* kids' band all day.

👍 Like 💬 Comment

C **UNDERSTAND IRONY** **How did the people realize they had made a mistake? Which sentences in the posts are ironic (the opposite of what the person means)?**

D **Who do you think got the biggest shock? Why?**

E **GROUP WORK** **THINK CRITICALLY** **What do you think the following people said and did in each story: (post 1) the people getting married, (post 2) the uncle, (post 3) Jim and Dana? Why?**

2 WRITING

A **MAKE A STORY INTERESTING** One way to make a story interesting is to mix longer and shorter sentences. Look at how sentences of different length are used in the two extracts from the posts in exercise 1B on page 60.

> I planned it all out very carefully: Drive to Las Vegas on Friday (six hours) and then drive to Salt Lake City (four hours) the next morning. We'd drive the whole ten hours back on Sunday. And the plan worked!

> The place was packed, but no one was seated, which was weird. Then, even weirder, we saw the bride and groom standing around chatting with people. I told my husband I hadn't expected to see them until after the ceremony. Then it hit me.

B You can also follow these points to make a story interesting. Find an example of each point in the posts in exercise 1B on page 60.

1 Use a variety of narrative verb tenses in the past.

2 Use different linking and organizing expressions: *and, but, so, then, later, a few years ago*, etc.

3 Use different kinds of sentences: conditionals (*if*), relative clauses (*who, which*), time clauses (*when, after*), *There was/were*, reported and direct speech, etc.

C [PAIR WORK] **Improve the sentences to make the story more interesting. Use the information in parentheses ( ) and your own ideas.**

My friend rented a red car from Cars-For-U. She called me. She said she would meet me on Thursday at the mall. She said I should find the red car and wait for her. (time clauses, linking expressions, direct speech)

I went to the mall and found a red car with a Cars-For-U sign on it. I stood next to it. I waited for a very long time. Then my friend found me. (variety of verb tenses, time clauses)

She asked what I was doing by that car. She said it was the wrong one. She pointed to another red car. It was closer to the mall. Sometimes I have the best luck! (relative clauses, direct speech)

 WRITE IT

D [PLAN] **You're going to write a story about something unexpected that happened or about someone who made a mistake. Discuss some ideas with a partner. You can use the ideas in the box or your own ideas. The story can be true, or you can make it up. Then think about how you are going to set the scene, what dramatic effects you'll use, and what comments you'll make.**

| getting on the wrong bus or train | going to the wrong event | getting caught in bad weather |

E Write your story. Make sure you use a mix of longer and shorter sentences and a variety of narrative tenses, linking expressions, and grammatical constructions described in exercise 2B.

F [PAIR WORK] **Exchange stories. What are the most interesting things about your partner's story?**

REGISTER CHECK

In more specific, official contexts, use other reporting verbs, rather than *say* or *tell*.
*The couple **announced** their engagement on Thursday.*
*She **promised** she would meet me in the evening.*

6.5

TIME TO SPEAK
StorySLAM

A   **DISCUSS** Read the rules to a storytelling contest with the theme "The Unexpected." Then look at the pictures. How do they relate to the theme? Discuss with a group.

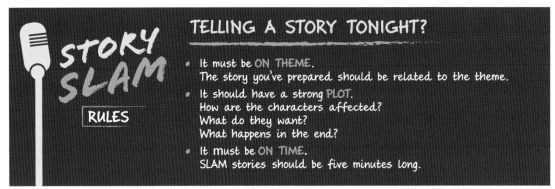

TELLING A STORY TONIGHT?

- It must be ON THEME.
  The story you've prepared should be related to the theme.
- It should have a strong PLOT.
  How are the characters affected?
  What do they want?
  What happens in the end?
- It must be ON TIME.
  SLAM stories should be five minutes long.

Now think of stories for each of the pictures with your group.

B   **PREPARE** You're going to tell a story for the StorySLAM with the theme "The Unexpected." It can be about yourself, someone you know, or someone you've heard about. Share a few ideas with a partner. Help each other choose the best story to develop. You can use one of the ideas from part A or your own idea.

FIND IT

C   **RESEARCH** How can you make a story interesting and lively? With your partner from part B, think of ways for the categories below. You can look online for help. You may want to watch some videos of storytellers. Then choose one or two of your ideas and use them to make your story more interesting.

details   language   tone of voice   gestures

D   **DECIDE** Tell your story to a group. The group considers these questions and chooses the best story: Did the storyteller follow the rules? Which story was the most interesting? Which storyteller was the liveliest?

E   **PRESENT** The winners from part D tell their stories to the class. The class chooses the best story.

To check your progress, go to page 154.

USEFUL PHRASES

DISCUSS

Looking at the picture, I'd say …

It could be a story about …

Maybe what happened was …

RESEARCH

You can catch the listeners' attention by …

I suppose you can …

It's entertaining to …

This website said that …

Another website claimed that …

REVIEW 2 (UNITS 4–6)

1 VOCABULARY

A **Complete the conversation with the correct expressions. There is one expression you won't use.**

acts as	constructive	contributes	draws attention to	keep an eye on
panic	point out	regain control	steer me away from	strengths
think through	turn to	weaknesses		

A Who's the most important person in your life?

B There are so many important people in my life, for example, my parents. They ¹_____ me and always ²_____ making bad decisions. That's important. But then there's my older sister. When I do make a mistake, she's the first to ³_____ what I did wrong. It makes me mad, but then she encourages me to ⁴_____ the situation and learn from it. And she gives me ⁵_____ advice.

A That seems rational.

B Yeah. When I have a problem, I tend to ⁶_____. She helps me calm down and ⁷_____.

A It sounds like she ⁸_____ your therapist!

B Yes, I guess she does in a way. Oh, and I can't forget my friend Dave. He ⁹_____ to my overall happiness. He always ¹⁰_____ my ¹¹_____, which makes me feel good. I can always ¹²_____ him to make me feel better.

B PAIR WORK **Who in your life is similar to the people described in exercise 1A? What other people are important in your life? Why?**

2 GRAMMAR

A Ⓒircle the correct options.

HOME　ABOUT　NEWS　BLOG　CONTACT US

Have you ever heard the expression "claim to fame"? It's that thing that makes someone famous or interesting. For truly famous people, it usually involves talent. For example, Shakira's claim to fame isn't ¹*only / even* her voice. People think of her voice *and* her dance moves ²*unless / whenever* they hear her name. For ³*others / one another*, it's often something silly or unusual. My brother's claim to fame is doing magic tricks. He would practice in his room ⁴*by himself / by herself* for hours as a child before he showed the family. ⁵*Providing / Even if* he's in a good mood, he still likes to show off his tricks today. He does this ⁶*such / so* often that everyone expects it now. And he does the tricks ⁷*only if / even if* he knows we've all seen them before. I think it's annoying, but the two of us always annoy ⁸*each other / the others*.

💬 2　♡ 7　🔁 11

B PAIR WORK **Answer the questions. Give details.**

1 Providing you're in a good mood, what's something you often do?

2 Do you have a claim to fame? Is it something you do by yourself or with others?

3 Is there something you do even if you know people don't like it?

3 VOCABULARY

A **There is one error in each sentence. Find and replace the errors with the words in the box.**

> argue   claims   happy   have   headlines   make   passionate   praises

1 I'm more than unwilling to help my friends when they need it because it makes me feel good.
2 I am no desire to try extreme sports. They scare me to death.
3 I'm not interested in celebrities who always want to be in the publicity.
4 I don't enjoy being around people who propose.
5 I don't believe it when an ad denies their product is the best. That's why I read the reviews.
6 I'm reluctant about traveling to other countries. I love experiencing other cultures.
7 One of my dreams is to do an appearance on a TV talk show or game show.
8 When someone boasts me, I feel pleased but also a little embarrassed.

B **PAIR WORK** **Do you agree with the sentences in exercise 3A? Why or why not?**

4 GRAMMAR

A (Circle) **the correct options.**

If you want to go on a cheap vacation, you ¹*should try / won't try* a virtual trip. There are many websites that offer virtual vacations you can take from your couch. For some of them, all you need is a computer and some time. One website ²*denied / boasted* that you ³*would feel / are feeling* like you were there – without ever leaving the house. Even if it's not as good as a real vacation, a virtual vacation ⁴*could make / can't make* you feel relaxed. One VR travel company ⁵*hopes to / claims that* you ⁶*enjoyed / might enjoy* a VR vacation more than a real trip because you don't have to deal with travel. If you take a lot of virtual trips, you ⁷*shouldn't learn / may learn* about amazing places around the world. But some people ⁸*told / argue* that a VR trip ⁹*would be / wouldn't be* the same as going to a new place.

B **PAIR WORK** **Would you try a virtual trip? Why or why not? What are the advantages and disadvantages? Discuss the questions with a partner. Then work with another pair and say how your partner answered the questions.**

GRAMMAR REFERENCE AND PRACTICE

1.1 PRESENT HABITS (PAGE 3)

Present habits

Talk about present habits in different ways:

1 Simple present (sometimes with adverbs of frequency)
*My friend **tells** me she **resists** change because she **usually likes** things the way they are.*

2 *Tend to* + the base form of a verb
*I **tend to adapt** to new situations quickly.*

3 *Will* for events that happen often (present, not future)
*I'**ll** often **call** my parents when I want advice.*

4 Present continuous for a continuing activity that happens at the same time as another habit
*I usually listen to music when I'**m cooking**.*

5 Present continuous for noticeable/unusual (often undesirable) habits; use *always* and *constantly* for emphasis.
*I'**m always worrying** about how I'll cope with all of my work.*

A Cross out the options that are <u>not</u> correct. Sometimes both options are correct.

1 I usually forget all about the time when *I'm studying / I will study*.

2 *I'll often take / I tend to take* a shower in the morning unless I have to leave home early.

3 I *never listen / am constantly listening* when he complains about his job.

4 My friends *often tell / are always telling* me to stop working so hard.

5 How do you communicate with people when *you'll travel / you're traveling*?

6 *I'll usually think / I usually think* about a task for a few days before I start on it, unless it's urgent, of course.

1.2 PAST HABITS (PAGE 5)

Past habits

There are different ways to talk about habits, actions, and states that happened in the past but don't anymore:

1 *Used to* for past habits, repeated past actions, and states
- *used to / didn't use to* + the base form of the verb
*We **didn't use to make** video calls, but we do now.*
- *never* + *used to* + the base form of the verb
*They **never used to ride** their bikes to school.*
- *use to*, not *used to*, with *didn't/did* in negative statements and questions
***Did** you **use to take** the bus?*

2 *Would* for past habits and repeated past actions, <u>not</u> for past states
- *would ('d) / would not (wouldn't)* + the base form of verb
- Use *would* only if it is clear when the action happened. Use *used to* if the time reference is not given.
*We **would text** each other every night.*   <u>not</u> ~~I would have a big cell phone.~~

3 The simple past for past habits, repeated past actions, and past states (often with time expressions)
*I **had** a big bedroom. I **went** to bed at 6:00 **every night**.*

4 The simple past for single completed actions in the past, <u>not</u> *used to* or *would*
*I **watched** three shows **last night**.*   <u>not</u> ~~I'd watch three shows last night. / I used to watch three shows last night.~~

A Change the simple past to *would (not)* when possible. When not possible, use *(not) used to*.

When I was young, I ¹<u>didn't have</u> a TV in my room. My older brother ²<u>had</u> one in his. I ³<u>was</u> very jealous. But on the weekends, he ⁴<u>let</u> me watch his TV. We ⁵<u>watched</u> our favorite shows, but I usually ⁶<u>fell</u> asleep halfway through.

2.1 COMPARATIVE STRUCTURES (PAGE 13)

Comparative structures

1 *Fewer/less* + noun to show there is less of one thing than another
   - *fewer* + count nouns   *less* + non-count nouns
   *The new project will require **fewer resources** and **less time**.*

2 *Rather than* to show a preference for something
   - Compare nouns/pronouns
   - Use verbs to compare activities (base form of the verb or verb + *-ing*)
   - *To* can be used instead of *rather than* with *prefer* but not with other verbs
   *I prefer ocean exploration **rather than space exploration**.*
   *I prefer to study the ocean **rather than learn**/**learning about** space.*
   *I **prefer** the ocean **to** deep space.*
   *I **want to study** Earth **rather than** Mars.*   not *I **want to study** Earth **to** Mars.*

3 Verb + *more/less* (as a pronoun)
   *I **know less**/**more** about Venus **than** about Mars.*

4 Adjective + (*not*) *enough* + infinitive to compare the degree of actual and required ability
   *Technology is (**not**) **advanced enough to send** people to Mars.*

5 A comparative + infinitive to compare actions
   *It's **easier** to use a tablet **than** (to use) a laptop.*

6 For many comparative structures, you do *not* need to repeat the first subject and verb.
   *We're **less likely** to find life on the moon **than** (we are to find life) on Mars.*

A **Complete the sentences. Use constructions from the grammar box above.**

1 We haven't been lucky _____ to see a whale in the ocean.

2 Larry prefers sea animals _____ land animals.

3 We see _____ turtles on the beach than in the ocean. There are many more of them in the ocean.

4 Scientists know _____ about Venus than about Mars. Venus hasn't been explored as much.

5 Vicky wants to work with animals _____ people.

6 It's _____ difficult to memorize dates than it is to remember names.

2.2 SUPERLATIVE STRUCTURES; UNGRADABLE ADJECTIVES (PAGE 15)

Superlative structures

1 With quantities: Phrases such as *one of, two of,* and *some of* + superlative adjective + plural noun
   *This country has **some of the highest** mountains in the world.*

2 With *to*: Use a superlative + infinitive to show function or purpose.
   *May is **the best** time **to hike** here.*

3 *Least* is the opposite of *most* (the comparative form is *less*).
   *This is surely **the least suitable** environment for anything **to live**.*

4 With *that* clauses:
   - Use a superlative + a *that* clause.   - The use of *that* is optional.
   *It's **the most fascinating** place (**that**) I've ever visited.*

5 Ellipsis with *the*: Shows that one or more words have been left out to avoid repetition.
   *I have three sisters. Susana is **the youngest** (sister).*

Ungradable adjectives

1   Ungradable adjectives do not have different degrees and therefore don't usually have comparative or superlative forms.

   *They were **furious** and **exhausted**.*

2   With most ungradable adjectives, we can use intensifiers such as *absolutely, completely, totally,* and *utterly*.

   *The green parrots of Masaya Volcano are **totally amazing**.*

3   With other ungradable adjectives – for example, *male, female, married, single* – we don't use intensifiers.

   *My first dog was **male**, but the second one was **female**.*

> **!** Gradable adjectives have degrees and can be used with adverbs, such as *very, a little,* and *really,* but <u>not</u> with intensifiers like *absolutely, completely,* etc.
>
> *Those animals are **very tough**.*
>
> **Note:** *Really* can be used with both gradable and ungradable adjectives.

A   **Circle the correct option.**

1   I think your cat is very *male / cute*.

2   It seems like the worst place for birds *building / to build* their nests.

3   My friends were absolutely *furious / interesting*.

4   The weather is a little *cold / freezing* right now.

5   For many of us, snakes are probably the *less / least* lovable species.

6   The lion and the elephant are two *most / of the most* popular animals at the zoo.

3.1   RELATIVE PRONOUNS; REDUCED RELATIVE CLAUSES (PAGE 23)

Relative pronouns; reduced relative clauses

1   Relative pronouns are used to introduce relative clauses.

   that/which = for things, *that/who* = for people, *where* = for places, *when* = for times, *whose* = to show possession

   *My sister, **whose** children I often take care of, lives next door.*

   *Today is the day **when** we decide it's time for a change.*

2   Subject relative clauses can be reduced by omitting the relative pronoun and the verb *be*. You can't reduce object relative clauses.

   The following relative clauses are often reduced:

   ■   with *be* + an adjective

   ■   with *be* + past participle

   ■   with noun phrases

   *People **who are worried** about meeting strangers often get nervous at parties.* → *People **worried** about meeting strangers often get nervous at parties.*

   *The bus **that is parked** in front of the office is the one we'll take to the conference.* → *The bus **parked** in front of the office is the one we'll take to the conference.*

   *Steven, **who is a quick learner**, adapts easily to new situations.* → *Steven, **a quick learner**, adapts easily to new situations.*

A   **Cross out the words you can omit to reduce the relative clauses when possible. When not possible, write X.**

1   The company whose logo is an apple is famous around the world.

2   Vincent van Gogh, who was an introvert, painted landscapes and self-portraits.

3   The book that was published anonymously sold millions of copies.

4   Psychology, which is normally a popular subject, is not her favorite.

5   This is the restaurant where my brother works.

6   People who are interested in others are often good conversationalists.

3.2 PRESENT PARTICIPLES (PAGE 25)

Present participles

Present participle = verb + -ing

1 To shorten sentences that describe two events happening at the same time, use the present participle of the second verb after a comma. Do not use *and*.

*I often work **and listen** to music.* → *I often work, **listening** to music.*

2 In reduced relative clauses, use the present participle. Do not use the relative pronoun and the verb *be*.

*Look at all those **lemons that are growing** on that tree.* → *Look at all those **lemons growing** on that tree.*

A **Rewrite these sentences to shorten them or use reduced relative clauses.**

1 The mall is full of people who are shopping for the holidays.

_____

2 We're standing in line and waiting to check in for our flight.

_____

3 There are a lot of fans who are waiting outside the stadium.

_____

4 I love to stand on top of that hill and look down at the valley.

_____

5 In college, I saw a guy who was skateboarding down a hallway.

_____

6 The storm will affect people who live in the South.

_____

4.1 ADDING EMPHASIS: *so … that, such … that, even, only* (page 35)

Adding emphasis

1 *So* + adjective or adverb *(that)* … emphasizes the results or effects of something.
*It was **so funny (that)** I couldn't stop laughing.*

2 *Such (a/an)* + (adjective) noun *(that)* … also emphasizes the results or effects of something.
*She is **such a good friend (that)** everyone turns to her when they have a problem.*

3 *Even* before a word, phrase, or part of the sentence adds emphasis or signals that something is surprising.
***Even** the most confident person needs help sometimes.*
*He works long hours during the week and **even** works on Saturdays sometimes.*
*Building trust with people makes your life **even** happier.*

4 *Only* before a word, phrase, or part of the sentence adds emphasis.
  ▪ *only* = "no one else" or "nothing else" than the people, things, amount, or activity mentioned
***Only** you can steer him away from making a big mistake.*
*Quitting your job will **only** hurt your career.*

A **Complete the sentences with *so, such, even,* or *only*.**

1 It was _____ a big decision to move to Canada and start over again.

2 _____ a very intelligent person can do that job.

3 She is _____ ambitious that she has decided to work toward a PhD.

4 Everyone was on time, _____ Joseph, who is usually late for class.

5 It was time to leave, but they had _____ packed one of their suitcases.

6 He demonstrated _____ talent that they hired him immediately.

4.2 REFLEXIVE PRONOUNS; PRONOUNS WITH *OTHER/ANOTHER* (PAGE 37)

Reflexive pronouns

Use a reflexive pronoun:

1 when the subject and object of a sentence are the same
*I enjoyed **myself** at the party.*

2 directly after a noun or pronoun for greater emphasis
*The employees **themselves** decide what time they start and finish work.*

3 at the end of the clause for some emphasis
*You and your brother should be able to do the job **yourselves**.*

4 after *by* to mean "alone" or "without help"
*I can't lift this box **by myself**.*

> **!** ***You*** **has two reflexive pronouns:** *yourself* **(singular) and** *yourselves* **(plural).**

Pronouns with *other/another*

1 *the other* = the remaining member of a pair
*One of his shoes was blue, **the other**, brown.*

2 *another* = an additional member of a group
*I'd like to hire **another** assistant.*

3 *the others* = the remaining members of a group
*Six people in my class are from this city. **The others** are from different cities.*

4 *others* (without *the*) = not the members of the group already mentioned, but different ones
*Some people drink coffee. **Others** prefer tea.*

5 *each other* and *one another* = show that each person in a group does something to the others
*During exams, students are not allowed to help **each other** / **one another**.*

A **Complete the sentences with the correct reflexive pronouns or pronouns with *other/another*.**

1 We knew it was going to be a tough job, but we told _____ we could do it as a team.

2 Do you and Antonio need help moving your furniture, or can you do it _____?

3 I know you already have two roommates, but is there room in your apartment for _____?

4 Come on guys, work as a team! Help _____!

5 My job involves a lot of teamwork, so I'm used to working with _____.

6 I was fixing the ceiling light and almost fell. I had one foot on a chair and _____ on the table.

5.1 REAL CONDITIONALS (PAGE 45)

Real conditionals

1 Present: *if/when/whenever* + simple present + simple present in the main clause
   - to describe general facts or routines
     *I **feel** nervous **if/when/whenever** I **think** about flying.*

2 Future: *if/when/whenever* + simple present + *will* / *be going to* in the main clause
   - for possible future situations and their results
     ***If** you **try** the therapy, it **will make** you more confident.*
     (You may or may not try the therapy. But if you do, it will make you more confident.)

     ***When/Whenever** you **try** the therapy, it **will make** you more confident.*
     (You will try the therapy, and when you do, it will make you more confident.)

3 With modals and modal-like expressions: *if* clause + a modal in the main clause
   - to show how likely or necessary the result is
     ***Whenever** you're worried, you **have to** try not to panic.*

Add the words in parentheses ( ) to the correct places in each sentence. Use a capital letter when necessary.

1   I arrive at the airport, I call you right away. (when, will)

2   Max anxious he sees a plane. (feels, whenever)

3   That app really helps people exercise, I buy it. (if, may)

4   I face my fear of heights I go over that bridge. (have to, whenever)

5   Everyone take off their shoes they want to enter that building. (must, if)

6   We take a trip to France your French improves. (can, when)

5.2   CONDITIONALS: alternatives to *if* (page 47)

Conditionals: alternatives to *if*

You can use real conditionals with expressions other than *if*, but they have different meanings:

1   *Even if*: Stresses that the condition doesn't matter. The condition may happen, but the result will be the same.
*   ***Even if*** *video calls improve, talking in person is much nicer.*

2   *Only if, providing / provided (that), as/so long as, on condition that*: Show the result or effect will happen when a specific condition becomes true. No other condition will have this result.
*   *I'll lend you my phone,* ***only if*** / ***provided*** / ***providing*** / ***as/so long as*** / ***on condition that*** *you promise to return it soon.*

3   *Unless*: Describes a possible negative condition in the present or future = "except if" or "if … not."
*   *We can't reach an agreement* ***unless*** *you communicate more openly.*

A   **Circle the correct option.**

1   I'm willing to try virtual office meetings *providing / unless* the technology is reliable.

2   *On condition that / Even if* we meet in person, we may not be able to reach an agreement.

3   We'll leave at 3:00 *provided / even if* everyone is ready.

4   You shouldn't study late *unless / only if* it's absolutely necessary.

5   *Even if / So long as* the company makes a profit, the boss is happy.

6   He should be able to get into that college *as long as / unless* he gets unexpectedly bad grades in high school.

6.1   NARRATIVE TENSES (PAGE 55)

Narrative tenses

1   Simple past for the main completed events and situations in a story.
*   *He* ***became*** *famous when he* ***was*** *only 14.*

2   Past continuous (*was/were* + verb + *-ing*) for background activities in progress at the same time as the main event in the simple past.
*   *She* ***translated*** *what the president* ***was saying***.

3   Past perfect (*had* + past participle) for an event that happened before another event in the simple past.
*   *All my friends* ***went*** *to the concert, but I'***d forgotten*** *to buy a ticket.*

4   Past perfect continuous (*had* + *been* + verb + *-ing*) for an event that continued up to another event in the simple past. It shows the continuing nature of a past activity/situation leading up to a more recent past time.
   ▪ It can show a reason.   ▪ It can give background information.
*   *The band* ***had been playing*** *all night, so they* ***were*** *very tired.*
*   *I* ***had been dreaming*** *of being famous for years, and suddenly it* ***happened***.

A   **Complete the sentences with the verbs in parentheses ( ) in the correct tense.**

We were exhausted when we ¹_____ (reach) the town. We ²_____ (travel) for days! There, we ³_____ (interview) several people about what they ⁴_____ (see). As we ⁵_____ (travel) back, we ⁶_____ (hear) that the story ⁷_____ (already / go) viral.

6.2 REPORTED SPEECH WITH MODAL VERBS (PAGE 57)

Reported speech with modal verbs

1   Some modals change when the reporting verb is in the past:

will – would   *can – could*   *may – might*

"**Will/Can** you **help** me?" → *Jen asked me if I'd / I **could help** her.*

2   Some modals don't change, even if the reporting verb is in the past: *might, could, should, must*

"What **could** they do about traffic?" → *He wondered what they **could** do about traffic.*

> **!** Only change the tense of the main verb when the reporting verb is in the past tense.

A   **Complete the sentences.**

1   "We won't study space next week."   The teacher announced _____ .

2   "Everyone should study for the test. "   The teacher feels _____ .

3   "We may not have time to see a movie. "   Lisa explained _____ .

4   "Could the Tigers win the baseball game? "   Joe asked me _____ .

5   "When will you finish the project? "   My boss asked me _____ .

6   "I can play the piano well. "   I said _____ .

This page is intentionally left blank

VOCABULARY PRACTICE

1.1 FACING CHALLENGES (PAGE 2)

A Circle the correct option.

1 I usually *welcome / resist* change – unless it's dangerous, of course!
2 Many people *accept / get a grip* that they have a limit to what they can do.
3 I've never *been capable of / been frightened of* learning new things. I love it!
4 When I'm really busy at work, I can't *cope with / underestimate* other things. I'm too tired.
5 My dad used to tell me, "You need to *welcome / adapt* in order to be successful."
6 I *tackle / can't take* all this work. It's too much!
7 When I'm stressed, I tell myself to *get a grip / be a step forward* and deal with things.
8 My good friends often help me *underestimate / get through* difficult times.
9 They say it's hard to *survive / be capable of* in this city, but I'm doing fine!

B Complete each sentence with the correct word or phrase from the box.

accept	adapt	can't take	capable of
frightened of	step forward	tackle	underestimate

1 I'm afraid I'm not _____ doing a sales manager's job. I don't have the skills.
2 We told the police what happened, but they wouldn't _____ our explanation.
3 You usually _____ well to big changes in your life.
4 Congratulations on your graduation! It's a _____ in your life, and a big one.
5 Don't _____ your ability to face challenges. You've always been good at dealing with new things.
6 She's moving to the country because she _____ the pressure of city life anymore.
7 I have to _____ some boring jobs around the house this weekend. They have to be done.
8 My mom says I was _____ other people when I was a child. Actually, I was just shy.

1.2 DESCRIBING ANNOYING THINGS (PAGE 4)

A Cross out the word or phrase that does **not** work in each sentence.

1 This app always crashes. It *is infuriating / is awkward / drives me crazy*.
2 My little sister asks a lot of questions. It *gets on my nerves / drives me crazy / is hard to operate*.
3 This remote control is *complex / time-consuming / tricky*. I can't figure out how to record a show.
4 Old laptops *were awkward / were clumsy / lost my patience* because they were too big and never fit in a bag.
5 This door is *a waste of time / infuriating / frustrating*. It always makes a loud noise when someone opens it.

B Complete each sentence with the correct form of the words or phrases in the box.

be a waste of time	be hard to operate	complex
get on sb's nerves	lose patience	time-consuming

1 These drones _____. The remote controls aren't easy to use at all.
2 Our internet connection really _____. I can't stream any movies.
3 Jackie _____ over little things – like when people ask her the same question more than once.
4 Painting our house is _____. We've been working for hours, and we've only done one room.
5 These directions are _____. I can't figure out how to put this table together.
6 Playing that game on your phone _____. You should be studying.

2.1 SPACE AND OCEAN EXPLORATION (PAGE 12)

A **Complete each sentence with the correct word. There is one item you won't use.**

atmosphere	come across	investigation	launched	observe
resources	satellite	species	surface	

What's Mars like? The ¹_____ of Mars is very different from the air around Earth. For example, there's very little oxygen in it. From ²_____ images we can see that the ³_____ of Mars is covered with rocks and red dust, so Mars is often called the Red Planet. People haven't been to Mars, but they've ⁴_____ spacecraft to ⁵_____ and explore it. They haven't ⁶_____ any plant or animal ⁷_____ on the planet, but they've found ⁸_____, like water and iron.

B **Circle the correct option.**

Ocean ¹*exploration / atmosphere* is useful in many different ways. For example, scientists are making breakthroughs in medicine by ²*launching / observing* different ocean ³*species / investigation*. So it's important to ⁴*monitor / come across* the ocean waters to ⁵*preserve / use up* life there, not only for food ⁶*exploration / resources*, but also because we have so much more to learn from it.

2.2 THE NATURAL WORLD (PAGE 14)

A **Circle the correct option.**

1 We climbed to the top of the *pond / volcano* to admire the view.

2 Ants and rats are excellent *sea life / survivors*.

3 How many animals are *endangered / adaptable* in your country?

4 What other *creatures / territory* can you find in this area?

5 The frog's natural *form of life / habitat* is in or around water.

6 There's a huge variety of *plant life / environment* in the Amazon rainforest.

7 Box jellyfish, which are fairly common, are one of the most *poisonous / endangered* species on Earth.

8 Dinosaur bones give us clues to their *origins / animal life*.

B **Complete each sentence with the correct word or phrase. Use each option only once.**

adaptable	animal life	forms of life	pond
survivors	sea life	territory	

1 Animals and birds try very hard to protect their _____.

2 Foxes are good _____ in both the city and the countryside.

3 There are many more _____ on Earth than we know of.

4 Unfortunately, there isn't much _____ in this forest anymore.

5 There's something swimming on the surface of the _____.

6 Ants might be small, but they are _____ creatures that can live in many environments.

7 Fish are one of the most common forms of _____.

3.1 DESCRIBING PERSONALITY (PAGE 22)

A **Match the words (1–5) with their definitions (a–e).**

1 show off _____   a talk and do things with other people

2 speak up _____   b try to get attention

3 extrovert _____   c someone who is shy and quiet

4 interact _____   d an energetic person who enjoys being with other people

5 introvert _____   e to speak in a louder voice so that people can hear you

B   **Circle the correct option.**

My sister and I often go out together. She likes meeting new people and ¹*enjoys the company of / shows off* strangers, but I prefer to hang out with people I know. She loves to ²*feel left out / socialize* in any environment, but I need to feel comfortable before I ³*interact / speak up* with people. When people invite us to their homes, she's ⁴*reserved / the life of the party*, and everyone loves her stories and jokes. I tend to ⁵*speak softly / speak up* and often ⁶*feel left out / attract attention* because I feel that no one wants to hear my stories. Sometimes, I think she ⁷*shows off / interacts*, but I guess that's not really true. I'm probably just a little jealous. The truth is, I never ⁸*am reserved / speak up*. If I did, everyone would probably listen to me, too. It's OK – if I find one person to talk to, I'm perfectly happy.

3.2 STRONG FEELINGS (PAGE 25)

A   **Complete each sentence with the correct word. Sometimes there is more than one possible answer.**

bizarre	creepy	disgusting	fabulous	impressive	irritating
satisfying	stunning	tense	uneasy	weird	

1   My internet connection has been slow lately. It's really _____ .

2   We saw some strange species of insects in the forest. They were like aliens – really _____ .

3   Having worked so hard painting the apartment, it was extremely _____ to see the results.

4   I'll never eat in that restaurant again. The food was absolutely _____ !

5   I felt confident in the interview but not before it. Before it started, I was really _____ and couldn't relax.

6   This landscape is _____ ! Let's take some pictures before it gets dark.

7   I used to get scared going into that old house. It was such a(n) _____ place.

8   We had a wonderful time on the coast. It was a(n) _____ weekend.

B   **Cross out the word that does not work in each sentence.**

1   From our hotel balcony, we could see the ocean. The view was *fabulous / uneasy / stunning*.

2   Cheryl thinks spiders are *creepy / disgusting / fabulous*, but she likes snakes.

3   I think it's *satisfying / weird / bizarre* that John can't stand the feel of plastic.

4   I always feel *tense / uneasy / irritating* when I have to speak in public.

5   Martin's new car is *tense / impressive / stunning*. I wish he'd let me drive it.

6   It was *an irritating / a tense / an impressive* situation, but we got through it.

4.1 PROFESSIONAL RELATIONSHIPS (PAGE 34)

A   **Circle the correct option.**

1   I think they need to *build trust / demonstrate* before they start that project.

2   Can you tell me who *oversees / acts as* student registration?

3   I had a difficult time at first because I had no one to *take on / turn to*.

4   The adviser at my college *enabled me to / contributed* get my first job.

5   My mother *steered me away from / kept an eye on* a lot of trouble when I was a child.

6   We want you to *build a relationship / assist* the general manager as soon as you can.

B   **Complete each paragraph with the correct words in the simple past.**

| act as | build trust | enable me to |
| keep an eye on | steer me away from | take on |

My cousin Frederico [1]_____ my tutor when I was in college. He [2]_____ the responsibility of helping me study and prepare for exams. He [3]_____ all my work and [4]_____ making mistakes. We [5]_____ together, and I can honestly say that he [6]_____ graduate with good grades.

| assist | build a relationship | contribute |
| demonstrate | oversee | turn to |

Marina quickly [7]_____ with her students, and they [8]_____ her whenever they needed help. She [9]_____ them with their studies in every way and [10]_____ all their exam preparations. She [11]_____ useful suggestions and ideas at every staff meeting and always [12]_____ interest and enjoyment in her job as a teacher here. I'm sorry she's leaving, but I wish her all the best for the future.

4.2   ASSESSING IDEAS (PAGE 36)

A   **Circle the correct option.**

It can be hard to make decisions. It's not always easy to [1]*assess / draw* what the final [2]*aspects / consequences* might be. And even if it's possible to think [3]*out / through* everything in detail, ideas often have both good and bad [4]*aspects / strengths*. This sometimes forces us to [5]*be destructive / weigh the pros and cons*. Things get even more complicated if a decision has to be made as a team. Team members often point [6]*out / up* the problems with each other's ideas. This can cause problems. Success depends on the personal strengths and [7]*cons / weaknesses* of team members. Some people are good at expressing criticism in a positive, [8]*constructive / destructive* way. They are careful to [9]*draw / point* attention only to valid points. Others are not as careful. They can sound rude, and the results can be [10]*constructive / destructive* to team relationships.

B   **Cross out the word or phrase that doesn't work in each sentence.**

1   I think he was being too critical. A lot of his points were *destructive / valid / unreasonable*.

2   We need to *assess / think through / point out* this plan and decide if it will work.

3   I'm really concerned about the *aspects / consequences / weaknesses* of his proposal.

4   Can I just *draw attention to / weigh the pros and cons / point out* a possible problem?

5   The boss was pleased with my *unreasonable / valid / constructive* suggestions.

5.1   DEALING WITH EMOTIONS (PAGE 44)

A   **Circle the correct option.**

1   When planes land, I'm *scared to death / conscious of* an uneasy feeling among the passengers.

2   You need to *calm down / panic* and think clearly.

3   Do you think the therapist can *regain control / cure* my fear of spiders?

4   Right now, my *breathing technique / anxiety level* is low.

5   I was afraid to drive, but my mom helped me *be scared to death / overcome my fear*.

6   It's important to *be rational / be in control of* when faced with fear.

7   Do you think trying *therapy / an anxiety level* will help him?

B Complete each sentence with the correct word or phrase from the box.

be in control of	be rational	breathing technique	cure
panic	regained control	was scared to death	

1 After panicking for a few minutes, I _____ and started to relax.
2 Do you want to _____ your emotions when flying? If so, try our VR therapy.
3 The movie was so frightening. I _____ .
4 We're trying to _____ about the decision, but it will change our lives completely.
5 Try not to _____ about your driving test. Breathe deeply and relax.
6 She feels much better, but the medicine didn't completely _____ her cough.
7 You might feel more relaxed if you try this _____ .

5.2 WILLINGNESS AND UNWILLINGNESS (PAGE 46)

A Circle the correct options.
1 I'm *passionate / eager* to learn languages, but my friend has no *desire / intention* of learning another language.
2 My dad is *more than happy / reluctant* to help me study, but he is *against / eager* helping me write my essays.
3 Some of us are *dying / hesitating* to go camping, but others are *anxious / passionate* to stay at home and study for their exams.
4 It's great you're *prepared / unwilling* to meet us at the airport. We're *reluctant / dying* to see you again!

B Complete each sentence with the correct phrase.

am prepared to	am unwilling to	are anxious to	have no intention of
hesitated to	is against	is passionate about	are reluctant to

1 I saw he was in trouble, but I _____ help him. I didn't want to make the situation worse.
2 We _____ meet your new friends. We can hardly wait.
3 I hate flying and _____ getting on a plane ever again!
4 She _____ keeping fit. She runs ten kilometers every day.
5 Sorry, but I _____ work this weekend. I'm tired and need to rest.
6 My mother can repair anything. She _____ buying new things if she can fix the old ones.
7 They _____ leave their house because they're watching a soccer game on TV.
8 I _____ accept the job if the salary is good enough.

6.1 TALKING ABOUT FAME (PAGE 54)

A Circle the correct option.

Jason [1]*had a good reputation / got hits* as a music student in college. One of his performances [2]*caught the media's attention / made an appearance*, and he soon [3]*heard of it / was getting a lot of publicity*. He never intended to [4]*seek fame / praise himself*, but he enjoyed the attention. After that, he [5]*raised awareness / made appearances* on several TV shows. I noticed he [6]*did the broadcast / made headlines* almost every day, so I went to one of his concerts. Jason really [7]*raised my awareness of / caught my attention* the power of music.

B Cross out the expression that does not work in each sentence.
1 The singer's videos *got a lot of publicity / got a lot of hits / made an appearance* in a short amount of time.
2 As a young artist, he *praised / caught everyone's attention / sought fame*.
3 Our band *did a broadcast / has heard of / made an appearance* online.
4 Famous people often have a need to make *headlines / appearances in public / a bad reputation*.
5 The teacher *raised awareness of / praised / made them entertaining* our creative videos.

6.2 REPORTING VERBS (PAGE 56)

FIND IT

A **Match the words (1–12) with the definitions (a–l). Use a dictionary or your phone to help you.**

1	announce ____	**a**	not be sure of something
2	argue ____	**b**	promise
3	boast ____	**c**	talk too proudly about something connected with you
4	claim ____	**d**	guess the size, value, amount, cost, etc., of something
5	confirm ____	**e**	tell people new information
6	deny ____	**f**	say something is true
7	estimate ____	**g**	give reasons to support or oppose an idea, action, etc.
8	have doubts about ____	**h**	suggest a plan or action
9	hope to ____	**i**	say something is not true
10	insist ____	**j**	want something to happen
11	propose ____	**k**	say something must be done
12	swear ____	**l**	to say that based on evidence something is true

B **Circle the correct option.**

1 My friends often *boast / hope to / swear* about their good grades.

2 When will you *insist / announce / claim* your plans to sell the company?

3 I was happy that the report *confirmed / estimated / denied* my numbers were correct.

4 I know that John was at a concert last night, but he *insists / denies / proposes* it.

5 Jenny *denied / had doubts about / swore* she told me about the party, but she hadn't.

PROGRESS CHECK

Can you do these things? Check (✓) what you can do. Then write your answers in your notebook.

Now I can ...

☐ talk about facing challenges.

☐ talk about present habits.

☐ describe annoying things.

☐ talk about past habits.

☐ discuss issues and agree strongly.

☐ write an opinion essay.

Prove it

Use four words to describe how someone you know deals with challenges.

Write three things you do every day using three different forms.

Think of a tech item you don't like. Use four words to say why.

Write five things you used to do ten years ago. Use three different forms.

Complete the conversation with words that are true for you.

A *As for* _____ , *I think* _____ .

B *Overall,* _____ .

Look at your formal essay from lesson 1.4. Find three ways to make it better.

Now I can ...

☐ talk about exploration and research.

☐ use comparative structures.

☐ talk about life forms in different environments.

☐ use superlative structures and ungradable adjectives.

☐ exchange important information.

☐ write a description of an area.

Prove it

Complete the sentences.

1 *I think travel to outer space* _____ .

2 *Exploring the ocean floor* _____ .

3 *We need to preserve* _____ .

Compare living underwater in a submarine to living in outer space in a spacecraft. Use these words: *endangered, habitat, plant life, poisonous, territory.*

Write five "amazing facts" about the animal, plant, and sea life in your country.

Use superlative structures to describe the amazing facts you wrote above.

Someone wants to visit your country for the first time. Give them some important information to help plan the visit.

Look at your description from lesson 2.4. Find three ways to make it better.

Now I can ...

☐ describe personality.

☐ use relative clauses.

☐ talk about things I love or hate.

☐ use present participles.

☐ make and respond to requests.

☐ write a personal statement for a job application.

Prove it

Describe two people you know. How are their personalities different?

Complete these sentences.

My [family member], whose _____ , *is* _____ .

Winter is a time when _____ .

Write about a sight, sound, or smell you love and one you hate. Say how they make you feel.

Complete the sentences with present participles and your own ideas.

I'm just sitting here, _____ .

Animals _____ *are* _____ .

Write a short conversation where one person makes a request and the other person refuses at first but finally agrees.

Look at your personal statement from lesson 3.4. Find three ways to make it better.

PROGRESS CHECK

Can you do these things? Check (✓) what you can do. Then write your answers in your notebook.

UNIT 4

Now I can …	Prove it
☐ talk about my support team in life.	Write about two people you know and describe how they support you.
☐ use *so, such, even,* and *only* to add emphasis.	Write four sentences describing how easy, hard, or fun your daily life is. Don't forget to add emphasis.
☐ make decisions.	Write three sentences about how you assess ideas. Use *weigh the pros and cons, constructive, point out.*
☐ use reflexive pronouns and pronouns with *other/another.*	Write three sentences with examples of reflexive pronouns. Write one sentence with a form of *other* and one with *another.*
☐ discuss advantages and disadvantages.	Write about the pros and cons of job sharing.
☐ write a summary.	Look at your summary from lesson 4.4. Find three ways to make it better.

UNIT 5

Now I can …	Prove it
☐ talk about dealing with emotions.	Write sentences using each of these expressions once: *anxiety level, be scared to death, calm down, regain control.*
☐ use real conditionals.	Complete the sentences with your own ideas. *If I decide to travel, I'll* _____ . *I might* _____ *if* _____ .
☐ express willingness and unwillingness.	Complete the sentences. *I have no desire to* _____ . *I'm dying to* _____ .
☐ use alternatives to *if* in conditionals.	Write four sentences about communicating with people. Use *as long as, unless, even if, only if.*
☐ consider and contrast ideas.	Write about the pros and cons of studying online.
☐ write an online comment with examples.	Look at your comment from lesson 5.4. Find three ways to make it better.

UNIT 6

Now I can …	Prove it
☐ talk about fame.	Give definitions of these words: *broadcast, get hits, raise awareness.*
☐ use narrative tenses.	Look back over the last five years of your life. Describe how you came to be in your English class now from that point in your life. Use narrative tenses.
☐ use reporting verbs.	Which reporting verb means: Say something is not true? Say you plan to do something? Say you want someone to do something?
☐ use reported speech with modals.	Change these sentences to reported speech. Julian announced, "I'll be famous some day!" A website claims, "The owner of Amazon is the richest man in the world." My sister insisted, "We can sing well."
☐ make assumptions.	Imagine your friend took a vacation abroad. Write six assumptions about what their trip was like. Then write their reply to each one. Imagine some of your assumptions were totally correct, some were partly correct, and some were incorrect.
☐ write an interesting story.	Look at your story from lesson 6.4. Find three ways to make it better.

PAIR WORK PRACTICE (STUDENT A)

1.3 EXERCISE 3C STUDENT A

1 **Discuss smartphones with Student B. Give your opinions about the issues below.**
Issues:

- easy or difficult to set up?
- good camera?
- usefulness of pre-installed apps?
- large enough screen?
- enough battery life?

2 **Listen to Student B's opinion about laptops. Say if you agree strongly or give your own opinion on the issues.**

2.3 EXERCISE 3B STUDENT A

1 **Student B will ask you for advice about buying a backpack. Use the information below to advise them.**
The backpack should:

1 be comfortable (very important)
2 be light
3 be the right size for you
4 have a waterproof cover
5 have a belt to go around your waist

2 **Then ask Student B for some advice about what kind of clothing to take on a skiing trip. Also ask about what kind of gloves to take. Your hands get cold easily, and you're worried about this.**

3.3 EXERCISE 3C STUDENT A

1 **Ask Student B for a favor:**
Conversation 1
You want them to be your guest at a company party this weekend.

2 **Listen to Student B, and for each refusal, use these cues to respond:**

- the people are nice and very friendly
- there will be good food, games, and music
- bring nephew; some coworkers have kids; kid-friendly activities are planned; he'd love it

3 **Student B is going to ask you for a favor. Listen and use the cues below to respond.**
Conversation 2

- refuse; you don't really like dancing
- refuse again; you're too shy; you'd be embarrassed
- refuse again; it's probably too expensive
- accept in the end

4.3 EXERCISE 3B STUDENT A

You're going to discuss open-plan offices (offices where all employees work in one big room). Tell your partner these advantages and disadvantages. Listen to their ideas.

Advantages:

- makes teamwork easier and increases creativity
- encourages people to work harder because they see others working

Disadvantages:

- is so noisy that it's difficult to work
- others can hear your work calls

5.3 EXERCISE 3C STUDENT A

1 **Imagine you like swimming. Tell your partner about its good and bad sides. Say how certain you are.**

+ Being in water keeps you cool.
+ A swimsuit is usually pretty cheap.
+ It doesn't hurt your knees and ankles.

– Chlorine from the water is hard on your skin.
– You have to pay to use the pool.
– You can get an ear infection.

2 **Now listen to your partner. They will tell you about the good and bad sides of running.**

3 **Compare your sports.**

PAIR WORK PRACTICE

6.1   EXERCISE 4A   STUDENT A

A   **You're going to tell a story about becoming famous quickly. Read the story quickly. Then read it again and underline key points. Pay attention to verb tenses. Then tell your partner the story in your own words.**

K-Pop Rocks

South Korean band Monsta X started in 2015 and became instantly famous for their synchronized choreography and unique mix of hip-hop, pop, and electronic dance music. The band had formed when its members participated in a TV talent show. Their first U.S. performance was in Los Angeles in 2015, but it was their first studio album with the title song *Beautiful* that reached number one in the Billboard World Albums chart in March 2017. In April 2018 their Japanese single *Spotlight* received an official gold certification by the Recording Industry Association of Japan. Now almost everything they do goes viral; the fans want to know everything. Like, did you know that the band leader Shownu loves dancing, is a good swimmer, and can pick things up with his toes? And Wonho, the lead singer and dancer, has acrophobia (fear of heights).

B   **Give your opinion of the stories.**

1.3   EXERCISE 3C   STUDENT B

1   **Listen to Student A's opinions about smartphones. Say if you agree strongly or give your own opinion on the issues.**

2   **Discuss laptops with Student A. Give your opinions about the issues below.**

Issues:

- size OK?
- weight OK?
- fast enough?
- enough battery life?
- usefulness of pre-installed software?

2.3   EXERCISE 3B   STUDENT B

1   **You want to buy a new backpack. Ask Student A for some advice. Also ask about using the backpack in the rain. You're concerned that stuff inside it will get wet.**

2   **Then Student A will ask you for advice about what kind of clothing to take on a skiing trip. Use the information below to advise them.**

Things you'll need:

1   a ski jacket (very important): thick, waterproof, strong

2   snow pants

3   ski goggles to protect your eyes (large sunglasses)

4   a warm hat

5   ski gloves: thick, waterproof, long enough to cover your wrists

3.3   EXERCISE 3C   STUDENT B

1   **Student A is going to ask you for a favor. Listen and use the cues below to respond.**

Conversation 1

- refuse; you don't know anyone
- refuse again; you don't think you'd enjoy it
- refuse again; you might have to take care of your ten-year-old nephew that day
- accept in the end

2   **Ask Student A for a favor:**

Conversation 2

You want them to join the dancing class you teach (decide the kind of dancing).

3   **Listen to Student A, and for each refusal, use these cues to respond:**

- it's really fun; they will love it
- dancing will make them more confident and outgoing
- it's not expensive; you'll give a big discount

PAIR WORK PRACTICE (STUDENT B)

4.3 EXERCISE 3C   STUDENT B

You're going to discuss open-plan offices (offices where all employees work in one big room). Tell your partner these advantages and disadvantages. Listen to their ideas.

Advantages:

- can encourage introverted employees to interact
- can save the company money

Disadvantages:

- people tend to waste more time because it's easy to talk to others
- can cause stress, especially for employees used to having a personal office

5.3 EXERCISE 3   STUDENT B

1   **Listen to your partner. They will tell you about the good and bad sides of swimming.**

2   **Now imagine you like running. Tell your partner about the good and bad sides of your sport. Say how certain you are.**

   + It's a good way to get outdoors.
   + You don't have to pay to use sports facilities.
   + You can listen to music while you're running.

   – In hot, cold, or wet weather, it's not much fun.
   – Good running shoes can be expensive.
   – It can be hard to find quiet routes without people and traffic.

3   **Compare your sports.**

6.1 EXERCISE 4A   STUDENT B

A   **You're going to tell a story about becoming famous quickly. Read the story quickly. Then read it again and underline key points. Pay attention to verb tenses. Then tell your partner the story in your own words.**

DIY Style

Wengie has been entertaining her friends for years, but she's only been a famous YouTuber for a short time. She was born in China and has lived in Australia since she was a child. She started writing one of Australia's top blogs, called the Wonderful World of Wengie, in 2011. She later started a YouTube channel that now has more than 11 million viewers. Her videos have gotten over 50 million hits. She gives tips on fashion and makes videos showing people how to make DIY (do-it-yourself) projects, such as colored pencils and holiday gifts. She had worked in a business office before she became a famous blogger and YouTuber. She gave up a well-paying job to follow her dream. Now she makes appearances around the world and is worth almost $2 million.

B   **Give your opinion of the stories.**

This page is intentionally left blank

This page is intentionally left blank

This page is intentionally left blank

This page is intentionally left blank

This page is intentionally left blank

This page is intentionally left blank

This page is intentionally left blank